IN
CONTROL

IN
CONTROL

NO MORE
SNAPPING AT YOUR FAMILY

SULKING AT WORK

STEAMING IN THE GROCERY LINE

SEETHING IN MEETINGS

STUFFING YOUR FRUSTRATION

**REDFORD WILLIAMS, MD,
& VIRGINIA WILLIAMS, PhD,**
authors of *Anger Kills* and *Lifeskills*

Printed in the United States of America
Rodale Inc. makes every effort to use acid-free ♾, recycled paper ♻.

Book design by Anthony Serge

Library of Congress Cataloging-in-Publication Data

Williams, Redford B., date.
    In control : no more snapping at your family, sulking at work, steaming in the grocery
line, seething at meetings, stuffing your frustration / Redford Williams and Virginia
Williams.
        p.   cm.
    Includes bibliographical references and index.
    ISBN-13 978–1–59486–256–4 hardcover
    ISBN-10 1–59486–256–7 hardcover
    1. Stress (Psychology)   2. Stress management.   3. Self-help techniques.   4. Life
skills.
    I. Williams, Virginia Parrott, date.   II. Title.
    BF575.S75W54   2006
    152.4—dc22   2005031229

Distributed to the trade by Holtzbrinck Publishers

2 4 6 8 10 9 7 5 3 1 hardcover

To Lucille Harris and Lawrence Harris

CONTENTS

ACKNOWLEDGMENTS

We gratefully acknowledge the help of the following people:

Mariska van Aalst worked closely with us from the beginning. She graciously accepted our invitation to visit for the weekend so the three of us could brainstorm different approaches. She went on to edit several drafts, always providing both helpful general comments and hands-on suggestions. She was, in short, an ideal editor.

Amy Super, who became our editor, worked with us diligently in the final stages of writing and production.

As with all of our books, Margaret Harrell provided indispensable help in reading all our drafts and offering detailed suggestions designed to clarify our thinking and reduce gracelessness.

Reid Boates, our ever-attentive literary agent, suggested this project to us. As usual, he stayed in contact, helping us throughout.

Sharon Brenner worked extensively early on to perfect the presentation of our program. Much of her work survives in this book.

Louise Koslofsky was Virginia's right-hand person. Her help was multidimensional, and she provided ideas and many details. In addition, her positive attitude in facing breast cancer during the genesis of this book demonstrated skillful behavior par excellence.

Jessica Sautter joined our office when the manuscript was near final editing. Reading with a fresh eye, she added invaluable observations.

Liz Kirby offered careful and thorough ongoing research on the effects of our coping skills training.

We'd also like to thank:

Barbara Barrett, who contributed much to our understanding of the police and their work

Jim Berryman, for suggestions to lighten as well as enlighten our text

Ann Bullock, for help with Cherokee-related matters

Matt Hocking, whose competent management of the research project freed Virginia from worrying about it

Janet Macaluso, for suggestions to soften assertion

Jennifer Phillips, for help in several matters

Nancy Meyer and Dave Salman, for information on organizational structures

Stephanie Nilsen and Susan Head, for their suggestions and insights over the years they worked with our program as coordinators of facilitators

Karen Weeks, an education specialist, for answering questions so we could disguise Margaret Polaski's real job

INTRODUCTION: LIFE'S WINNERS

Would you like to be more in control of your life? Of course!

Some people seem naturally able to achieve this. You rarely see them lose their cool. They almost never blow up. They don't descend into a gloom that leaves them isolated and miserable. Nor do they allow themselves to be stepped on. The result is that they exercise an unusual degree of control over themselves and their world.

ARE PEOPLE BORN IN CONTROL?

It's tempting to think, "Those people just have all the luck." In some cases, this may be true; some people were born that way. Others learned their skills by copying their parents. But is the winner's circle this limited? Does being in control of yourself and the world around you have to boil down to nature and nurture?

The truth is that both help, but others of us without these strengths aren't doomed. For over three decades at Duke University, Redford has been investigating the connections between mental states and body functions. He also has studied how genes figure into the mix. Colleagues at other medical centers around the world have been engaged in similar pursuits. One conclusion from all of this research is that people with certain personality traits are much more likely to be successful, content, physically healthy, and downright happy, regardless of their genetic material or upbringing. Almost by definition, they're also more likely to be in control.

These findings have led to another set of questions. Could behavior be learned? Could these personality traits be acquired later in life? Are there ways we and others can develop healthier profiles? As you'll see later on, one big impetus for addressing these questions was self-help. Redford's repeated angry outbursts were causing trouble at work and at home; Virginia's inability to assert her needs was causing rifts between the two of us. We had a great incentive to find a constructive way to gain greater control over ourselves and our lives—and fast!

We set about developing a system that could help even the most angry, depressed, or powerless people gain more control, while improving their health. As we fine-tuned this process, using ourselves as test subjects, we taught it to everyone from Fortune 500 money managers to inner city youth, from burned-out government workers to oppressed Native American tribes. In each case, we observed through both anecdotal evidence and independent clinical research that our process could help reverse depression, social isolation, and hostile feelings, while increasing self-esteem and social support. For example, in a group of people recovering from heart attacks, those who had received the training were still reaping tangible physical rewards 6 months later, such as lower blood pressure and 76 percent less time spent in the hospital (an average of only 0.6 day during those 6 months versus 2.5 days for those who hadn't received the training). Another group slashed depression by 60 percent!

You can learn the good habits that lead to better control by following our 8-week program in Part 2 of this book. As we go through each week, we'll look at examples of men and women who turned their lives around by learning the set of skills that enabled them to get control of their lives. Rather than being "born with it," these people mastered the techniques that helped them get their needs met, without offending others. Key relationships at home, work, and elsewhere were improved. As a result, these people became more productive, fulfilled, and happy. This in turn influenced their opportunities and gave them courage and self-confidence—the beginning of a revolution in their lives! They developed the key habit that people in control of their lives have: They know how to create the kind of success in their work, their home lives, and their relationships that continually breeds more success. You'll meet:

- A housewife who ate her way through every life crisis but learned to stop stuffing her feelings and her face
- An angry academic who pulled himself up out of a challenging environment, but then had to learn to control his temper
- A policeman who stopped letting the stress of his job harm his health and his relationships
- A career woman with a husband, teenage children, needful parents, and too much to do who regained a degree of control
- A Southern belle who finally learned to assert herself, rescuing her marriage and self-esteem
- An overburdened Cherokee schoolteacher who developed the knack of saying no and making it stick
- A timid civil servant who learned to champion herself and her favorite programs
- An executive who became pals with his teenage son again
- A grandmother who got back on track with her husband and a co-worker
- A high school teacher who finally learned how to make English literature exciting to his students

Some of these people needed to learn only one new habit to turn their lives around; others had to acquire several of the skills. Ultimately, theirs are just a few of the hundreds of success stories we've heard over the years. They're illustrations of what we know now: By following the 8-week program and thus gaining greater control of your life, you can change your destiny.

YOUR PATH BEGINS HERE

Regardless of where you are now, you can change your negative or self-destructive habits, and the skills you'll learn in the next 8 weeks will get you there. You'll learn to accurately read the world around you for clues to your best opportunities. You'll learn to react in ways that support your own needs and goals and elicit the responses you're looking for. You'll master the keys to self-control, and you'll learn to have a considerable degree of control over your environment as well. You'll learn to speak in ways that get you heard and improve all facets of communication with the people you care about the most. You'll even realize how liberating optimism can be and what a difference looking on the bright side can make in your life. In short, in many cases, you will get what you want, and even more important, you will get what you need.

And, yes, you may still slip occasionally—even the most effective people do. The goal is progress, not perfection.

One thing we won't ask you to do is spend a tremendous amount of time dredging through your past or considering the origins of your emotional challenge areas. Traditionally, if you sought help during a tough time, your treatment would include delving into the deep, hidden roots of your problems. Sometimes, what you learned gave you a clear idea of the sources of your difficulties, which was helpful. But the entire process could be very time-consuming and expensive, and ultimately, you might still lack the skills necessary for a great life.

Happily, we aren't alone in focusing on emotional health rather than on mental disturbances. As you'll learn in Chapter 1, hundreds of medical research projects conducted over the past several decades have demonstrated that winning attitudes improve physical health. Some of the most exciting current research examines the roots of resiliency and success. The conclusions are clear: We know the qualities that make people succeed, and the next winner could be you.

If you're eager to jump right in, turn to page 33 and take the Self-Assessment Quiz. This test not only shows you where you stand on the control continuum (from not at all to fully in control), it also tells you which of the skills will be your biggest challenge areas. Armed with that information, you can move on to Part 2 and the 8 weeks that will teach you the skills. You'll learn more about people who turned their lives around, and you'll do exercises that will help you improve.

Depending on your goals, you may want to read the book all at once or take one week at a time. No single approach is best for everyone. The skills you'll learn are cumulative, so to keep your momentum, decide on the approach that suits you, and change your strategy if and whenever necessary.

One thing is certain: No matter how you approach the program, simply by picking up this book, you've taken your first step toward gaining control and moving into a life filled with more purpose, connection, happiness, and health.

Now, are you ready? Let's get started!

PART ①

LIVE LONGER AND LAUGH MORE

CHAPTER 1

THE SCIENTIFIC PERSPECTIVE: THE SKILLS YOU'LL LEARN COULD SAVE YOUR LIFE

At first, Sarah McDonald* was aware of only the steady beep, beep, beep of the heart monitor above her head. Then, as she slowly opened her eyes, she was dazzled by the bright fluorescent lights of the cardiothoracic surgery recovery unit. As she adjusted to the glare, she could make out other patients lined up on gurneys to her left and right. Nurses and doctors were quietly going about the business of making sure their charges were doing okay.

Sarah panicked for a few seconds when she tried to talk and found she could produce only a low, inarticulate moan. A breathing tube had been placed in her throat to prevent aspiration in case she should vomit while coming out of anesthesia—a fact she now dimly recalled from the pre-op video. A dull ache pounded in her chest where her sternum had been split to provide access to her heart, so the surgeon could bypass the blocked arteries that had caused her heart attack.

Two days earlier, on New Year's Day, Sarah's normally undramatic heart had suddenly called attention to itself. The Christmas season had been hectic. Finally savoring the end of the marathon rush, she and her friend Liz were taking their regular morning walk. They moved along briskly, arms swinging in rhythm with each step. The frigid northwest wind, so familiar in this northern city where Sarah and her husband, Hal, had lived for 26 years, added to their workout.

---

* Unless otherwise indicated, throughout this book we have altered the names of individuals and key details of their stories to protect their privacy.

At first, the only sign that something was amiss was a "funny feeling" in her left ear. Then a sensation of coldness in her chest rose to a level and took on a quality she had never experienced before. "My chest feels cold," she said to Liz, trying not to be concerned.

"Yeah, mine, too," Liz answered, rubbing her hands together for warmth.

Sarah tried to ignore the strange sensation but succeeded for only a few moments. Then she broke into a profuse sweat, the beads quickly forming and running down her face. While she wouldn't have described the feeling in her chest as painful, it just felt strange. With alarming suddenness, the reality dawned.

"Oh, God," she thought. "It's my heart!"

"BAD STUFF" HARMS YOUR HEALTH

Over the past three decades, we at the Behavioral Medicine Research Center at Duke University and other researchers around the world have been engaged in work aimed at identifying the types of psychological stress—the "bad stuff"—that contribute to heart disease and other major illnesses. We know a great deal more than we did just 30 short years ago, and all of this research has had a hand in helping to reveal the strategies that people successfully use to stay in control.

In the 1970s, early research in this field suggested that people who had the type A personality—hurrying, hostile, impatient, and ambitious—were at higher risk of developing coronary heart disease. Later studies then seemed to contradict these findings: Only some type A's experienced this elevated risk. In the quest to find the reason, Redford and other behavioral medicine researchers discovered that a person could be ambitious, hurrying, and even impatient, yet wouldn't have a higher risk of heart disease. He and his colleagues were able to show that the key characteristic of type A that was damaging to health was *hostility*.[1]

This and other research revealed that people who felt a cynical mistrust of others, experienced frequent bouts of anger, and spoke or acted aggressively toward others were at higher risk not only for heart disease but also for a wide range of other life-threatening illnesses. One study centered on a group of doctors who had taken a personality test in medical school back in the 1950s. Of those with higher hostility scores, 14 percent were dead by age 50. Their mortality rate was *seven times higher* than that of those with low hostility scores.[2]

At this point, we had a clear indication that some of us court self-imposed distress, damaging our health as we grow older.

HOW THE "BAD STUFF" GETS INSIDE YOUR SKIN

Sarah walked quickly but carefully, as though on eggshells, to the front steps of the next house they approached. She asked the neighbor to call Hal, then sat on the steps until he arrived. After a brief discussion about whether to call 911 for an ambulance, they got in the car, and Hal drove her to the ER of the nearby community hospital. He pushed her in a wheelchair up to the reception desk, with both of them saying "Chest pain, chest pain!" loudly enough for all nearby to hear. She was quickly taken to a room and hooked to a heart monitor. A nurse came in and did an EKG.

Shortly, a doctor came in and told them that she was indeed having a heart attack, "a big one." Sarah talked through the entire attack, beginning with demands that the staff quickly give her the clot-busting drug TPA. She knew from her reading that it could stop a heart attack in its tracks.

"Well, where's that TPA?" she demanded.

The nurse knew that if Sarah got upset, it would only make matters worse. "They're mixing it up now," she said soothingly, placing a hand on Sarah's arm. Sarah shook it off. She wasn't buying the stalling tactics. "Get it now!" she yelled.

Compared with their more easygoing counterparts, people who are more hostile excrete much larger amounts of the stress hormones adrenaline and cortisol into the bloodstream when they become angry.[3] This causes other, potentially harmful biological changes inside the body.

- Blood pressure and heart rate surge, which can damage the lining of the coronary arteries. This is the first step in the formation of plaques that can lead to heart attacks years down the road.

- Fat cells dump large amounts of fatty acids into the blood. If these fats are not burned up by intense muscular exercise, the liver will process them into cholesterol, which also contributes to the formation of artery-clogging plaques.

- Immune system cells undergo changes in their functions, then collect in areas of arterial damage, where they also encourage plaque formation.

- The clotting mechanism of the blood is activated, further stimulating the development of arterial plaques. This activity may even trigger the final artery-blocking clot that results in a heart attack.

This response, called fight-or-flight, is often appropriate when you're confronted with true physical danger. If you're trying to get out of a burning building or fight off someone who's attempting to attack or kill you, you need this response to ensure your survival. But thankfully, real life-or-death situations are rare in most of our lives. In today's world, the stress response can be extremely counterproductive if you're just coping with a traffic jam or a boss who's treating you unfairly. All it accomplishes then is to increase the likelihood and the speed at which these processes produce clogged arteries—definitely some pretty bad stuff.

People who are in control of their reactions know how to save this major response for truly dangerous situations. Those in less control (like Sarah before she began her odyssey) turn it on for even the most trivial everyday annoyances.

So what separates these two types of people? Why are some people able to make the distinction between true danger and pointless anger, while others aren't? Research was telling us that distinct differences existed—some were biological, surely, but some were a matter of coping style. We realized that if we could develop a way to help people short-circuit the hostile impulses that were getting so many of them into emotional and physical trouble, we could help them develop new strategies that could save not only their relationships but also their lives. Part of that was isolating and articulating the secrets of the people who just naturally seemed to know how to control their hostility.

THE BIRTH OF IN CONTROL

More than a decade ago, we began by developing a set of strategies (described in our first book, *Anger Kills*) aimed mainly at helping people decrease their hostility and anger—the first bad stuff shown by Redford's research to harm the heart. This loose collection of strategies began to evolve into a more systematic training program, which we termed LifeSkills. In addition to trying to reduce the bad stuff, the LifeSkills workshop (described in our second book, *Lifeskills*) included a focus on the positive. The twin emphases were on damage control and damage prevention. The damage-control skills enable you to deal with conflicts and stress in your life and relationships. The damage-prevention skills aim to prevent bad stuff from occurring in the first place by improving how you treat yourself and others.

One follow-up study, done with employees of one of our corporate clients 6 months after the initial training, confirmed that our program accomplished more than simply reducing the bad stuff. Some in this group, which included workers at both managerial and support levels, had been experiencing problems at work, while others took the training to improve their already good skills. In the workshop, we taught them to evaluate and manage situations that bothered them and to interact more supportively and positively with others. The follow-up study showed that in addition to experiencing decreases in negative characteristics such as hostility, anxiety, and depression, the employees also showed increases in positive attributes such as social support and self-esteem.[4]

We recently began a study to determine whether similar results can be obtained by watching a video designed to teach the same skills as the workshop. The good news: In this ongoing study, we're finding that levels of depression, anxiety, and perceived stress all decrease as much in those trained with the video as in those who take the workshop.

Findings like these prodded us to formulate a new construct—In Control—that further shifts emphasis to those attitudes and actions that not only help people overcome their bad habits but also make them winners. People who are in control have certain skills that help them enjoy sustaining relationships, worldly success, a sense of well-being, and enhanced health. They've mastered the ability to accurately assess sticky situations, choose the right actions or reactions to get their needs met, and, *at the same time*, create an environment in which other people—family members, friends, and even co-workers—feel safe, loved, and encouraged to be and do their best.

Because they've gone from simply dealing with the bad stuff to optimizing the good, these people know how to shape their environments to create sustained joy and good feelings among most, if not all, people with whom they come into contact.

The Self-Assessment Quiz in Chapter 2 will help you gauge whether you presently possess the skills to be in control, where any challenge areas lie, and how much work, if any, remains to be done. This test is the culmination of years of fine-tuning our workshops, decades of clinical research, and many long hours thinking about what it means to be an emotionally healthy person in our sometimes shockingly unhealthy world. We've drawn inspiration from the key work of other pioneers in the field of biobehavioral health, and we've been gratified to see how all of this work fits together with our research.

MORE "BAD STUFF": HOSTILITY IS JUST ONE DANGER

Sarah's heart attack was years in the making. She had worked as a physical therapist ever since her three girls were old enough to take care of themselves after school, with her salary going directly into their college fund. She was nearly always heavily booked with patients, and she felt that many of her days were stressful. "I didn't work at a relaxed pace," she said.

Sarah thought about what she was like during those earlier years. She began to realize that her hurrying, hostile, ambitious type A nature had played a big role in her frequent feelings of distress. Her credo was "It's easier to depend on yourself to get things done, since others are probably going to screw up."

She never considered herself an angry person, but in retrospect, she realized she had spent a lot of time in a state of what she now knew was chronic annoyance at those who didn't measure up to her high standards. "That's what got my adrenaline pumping," she admitted.

Besides these self-imposed stresses, Sarah experienced plenty of other hardships that would be enough to stress anyone. Her mother had died of congestive heart failure 9 years earlier, at age 73, after struggling with heart disease and bypass surgery. But that was only the beginning of a very difficult period for Sarah. A year after her mother's death, her brother and father had a major argument over the brother's hatred of their father's girlfriend—a period in Sarah's life that was "as stressful as it gets," she said.

When that crisis finally ended, more difficulties followed. Her father's health declined rapidly, and Sarah and her sister took on the role of caregivers. He became less and less able to look after himself ("The house was a pigsty!" Sarah ranted). Eventually, they were forced to move him into an assisted-living facility. This led to another set of problems as he became increasingly demanding and manipulative.

Sarah felt her only effective response was to try to outsmart her father when he cried wolf every time something didn't go exactly his way. It wasn't until after her heart surgery that she was able, finally, to tell him, "I need to take care of me and live my own life." This stance helped her cope and appeared to help her dad cope, too. At some level, he seemed to realize that Sarah needed to be self-protective.

Luckily, through it all, Sarah knew that she had the love of her husband, whom she loved with all her heart. She came to recognize, however, that although he had many fine qualities, he was simply not the kind of person she could depend on to provide a sympathetic ear when the world weighed heavily on her. She was close to two of her daughters, but they had their own lives in other cities. Other than frequent phone chats, they didn't have as much contact as Sarah would have liked. The third daughter was of an independent mind—"her own person"—and wasn't a ready source of emotional support.

All in all, Sarah's life had been a roller coaster of emotion for as long as she could remember. As part of her recovery from the heart attack, she would have to learn how to manage her emotions—not only to save her relationships but also to save her life.

Hostility isn't the only negative trait that can have an impact on people's health. Behavioral medicine research has identified a number of other risk factors with a definite link to serious health problems.

Depression. The negative impact of depression also increases the risk of developing coronary heart disease, and people who are depressed after having a heart attack are more likely to die within the following 6 months.[5] Several studies have shown that patients with any disease—diabetes is one example—who are depressed end up needing more medical care, accounting for a disproportionate amount of medical costs.[6]

Lack of adequate social support. People who have little support—whether it's help with chores at home or someone to listen sympathetically—are also more at risk. Social support acts as a buffer that enables people to cope better with whatever stresses they face, whether they're imposed by personality or life situations.[7] Support is a function of both the person and the environment. Those of us who have a cynical mistrust of others are less likely to reach out for support, and some of us find ourselves in situations that simply don't include people who can be sources of support.

Stressful environments. Jobs that impose high demands for output of services or products but allow workers little control over how those demands are met have been termed high-strain jobs. Psychologists Robert

Karasek, PhD, of the University of Massachusetts, and Tores Theorell, MD, PhD, of the Karolinska Institute in Stockholm, Sweden, have documented that people working in high-strain jobs are more likely to develop high blood pressure, infections, and job-related injuries, as well as heart disease.[8]

Risky behaviors. People who are hostile, depressed, isolated, or in stressful life situations are more likely to overeat, smoke, and abuse alcohol.[9]

Studies show that these different risk factors often cluster in the same individual. For example, in a study of working women, Redford and his colleagues found that those who reported high job strain were also more depressed, hostile, and socially isolated.[10] As in people with high levels of hostility, these other psychosocial risk factors are associated with changes in biological functions, such as increases in adrenaline and cortisol, blood pressure and heart rate surges, higher cholesterol levels, and alterations in the immune system and blood-clotting mechanisms. All of these changes are felt to lead to disease.[11]

Redford's research has continued to build upon the observation that these risk factors, along with the accompanying biological markers of stress and health-damaging behaviors, tend to cluster among certain groups. The people most likely to be affected are those stressed by lower income, education, and/or occupational levels.[12] This clustering may be the result of reduced brain levels of the chemical serotonin, a neurotransmitter that nerves use to relay messages to one another. When serotonin levels are low, we are more likely to be angry, depressed, and anxious; to be less interested in relating to other people; to have greater fight-or-flight responses when stressed; and to smoke, drink, and eat more than is good for us. If true, this theory could point to the brain's serotonin system as a key neurobiological mechanism that regulates our ability to be in control. Two studies have found weaker brain serotonin function in persons with lower income and education levels.[13]

In his most recent research, Redford has begun to study how genes that are involved in regulation of serotonin affect all of these health-damaging psychosocial, biological, and behavioral characteristics. This work is still in an early stage, but we have some likely hypotheses for where it will go. The serotonin "transporter" is a molecule that sits on the surface of serotonin nerve endings. It's responsible for the reuptake of serotonin—squelching the effects of the neurotransmitter after it's been released from the nerve endings. The gene responsible for making this transporter comes in various forms. Certain of these forms seem to make a person more likely to experience negative emotions, such as anger and depression, and to have greater adrenaline, blood pressure, and heart rate surges when angered.[14]

Redford's ongoing work aims to identify the interactions between key genes and the environment and to help account for the clustering of health-damaging characteristics in the same individuals and groups. No doubt, we will also learn more about how genes affect our ability to be easily in control in stressful situations. Stay tuned for additional revealing research, but in the meantime, let's talk about how *you* fit in to this picture.

ARE YOU AT RISK?

Do you recognize similarities between Sarah's situation and your own life? Do you find yourself spending a lot of time each day feeling annoyed with others who behave in ways that get your goat? Do your job and family responsibilities create a stressful high-demand, low-control situation? Are you a member of the "sandwich generation," squeezed by responsibilities to both children and parents? Do you frequently notice signs of stress in your body? Perhaps your heart beats rapidly, or you breathe faster and more deeply. Maybe your palms sweat or your voice rises in pitch. Do you experience tightness in the muscles of your neck, back, and shoulders?

If so, it could be that like Sarah's, your adrenaline levels are high. If that's the case, your current control level may be too low to protect you against the stresses you face, whether they stem from your personality, your environment, or, as is often the case, both. You may want to pay particular attention in Weeks 1 through 5 of the program, as they can help you get control of your responses to stressful situations and formulate the right plans to get your needs met.

Fortunately, Sarah's control level was not stuck where it was prior to her heart attack—and neither is yours.

HEALING WITH EMOTIONAL EXCELLENCE

Finally, the TPA arrived, and the nurse was ready to start Sarah's intravenous drip.

Hal knew he would become woozy just watching the nurse insert the IV, so he decided to wait outside. Sarah's concern about how Hal was taking the situation turned out to be a potential problem in itself. Her cardiologist furrowed his brow and said, "When members of your family come in, your adrenaline goes up." He suggested that she have no visitors until her condition stabilized.

Over the next 24 hours, her medical workup moved forward and included a coronary arteriogram to determine if there were blockages in the arteries that supply blood to her heart muscle. She was surprised by the results of this test. "I never would have guessed I had five blocked arteries!" said Sarah, who was only 53.

The next day, after her bypass surgery, Sarah felt as if she'd been hit by the proverbial Mack truck. She hurt all over. Especially painful was the incision where her chest had been split. Even after she was moved out of intensive care, she was so exhausted that she couldn't even stand without assistance. Not surprisingly, her cynical worldview had an effect on her perceptions and behavior. "Remembering what my mother went through with inexperienced residents, I told them I wanted no students taking care of me," she said angrily. "But then I heard there were students!" She insisted that a No Visitors sign be placed on her door, and she was annoyed when this didn't keep friends and neighbors out. Instead of getting better, the ache in her breastbone worsened.

Fortunately, Sarah's aggression was not her only driving force. During the 10 days she spent in the hospital, her attitude remained upbeat. "The doctors and *nurses asked me to tell them if I felt depressed, but I was thrilled just to be alive!"* she said. Other factors also helped her stay positive, such as the "Notes on Sarah's Hospitalization" that Hal had recorded on his computer throughout the saga. Sarah was very touched when her normally reticent husband gave her the diary.*

Her daughters all rallied around her as well. In the hospital and after she returned home, they waited on her hand and foot. Sarah was grateful for the incredible bonding experience of her first few weeks at home. Even her oldest daughter, who had always been a bit distant, became devoted and continued calling her mother daily after returning to her home.

When the last daughter departed, the predicted depression did hit. One night while listening to classical music, Sarah cried for an hour. But to her credit, she didn't let the depression take hold. She drew strength and encouragement from the loving support she was receiving, and she took some positive steps to help herself.

Sarah went into cardiac rehab and began attending a support group with fellow heart attack patients. Her experiences there helped improve her coping skills, leading to a more sure sense of control in her life. "I could go and tell my story," she said. "I felt I could share, and they'd understand." She got back to her walks, and as she strode around the indoor track, she noted that most of the other patients in rehab were older. "I realized, 'They're in their eighties and making it through this—so can I!'" she recalled.

Sarah did one more thing to take control of her recovery and her life: As soon as she was up and about, she called the director of the medical facility where she had worked for all those years, all those days with full appointment schedules, and said, "I quit."

Sarah's postoperative experience reflects mounting evidence that shows both negative and positive attitudes can have a profound impact on prognosis in patients with life-threatening diseases.

The biological and behavioral mechanisms that appear to contribute to the development of heart disease take years to produce the artery-blocking plaques that eventually cause a heart attack. Once you've had a heart attack, however, the whole process can speed up, and a fatal outcome becomes much more likely. Among people who have had heart attacks, those with depression, anger, anxiety, and social isolation continue to have a worse prognosis.

A considerable body of research has made it clear that depression after a heart attack can have almost as big an impact on prognosis as congestive heart failure. One study in Canada found that patients who were severely depressed following heart attacks were five times more likely to die within 6 months (15 percent of those participants died) than patients who were not depressed (3 percent died).[15]

Social isolation also has a negative effect on outcome in heart disease. Redford and his Duke colleagues followed more than 1,300 heart patients. A full 50 percent of those who weren't married and said they had no one they could talk to about distressing matters died within 5 years, compared with only 18 percent of those who had a spouse, a confidante, or both.[16]

Now for the "Good Stuff": A Positive Life Improves Health

Behavioral medicine researchers are now beginning to realize that good health depends on more than simply reducing hostility, depression, social isolation, and job strain. For optimal health, you also need to have supportive social ties, positive emotions such as joy, an optimistic outlook, and confidence in your ability to cope with the stresses life throws at you. Spearheaded by University of Pennsylvania psychologist Martin Seligman, PhD, this "positive psychology" movement says that in order to prevent and treat disease and increase well-being, we must look beyond the historical focus on pathology (the bad stuff) and be equally concerned with enhancing qualities and experiences that make life more worthwhile (the good stuff).[17]

There is growing evidence that people who have a positive outlook enjoy better health overall and are less likely to develop major illnesses.

Studies by psychologists Michael Scheier, PhD, of Carnegie Mellon University in Pittsburgh; Charles Carver, PhD, of the University of Miami; and others have shown that optimists (people who believe things will turn out well) are:

- Half as likely as pessimists (those who expect things to turn out badly) to be rehospitalized following coronary bypass surgery[18]
- More likely to succeed in an alcohol abuse rehabilitation program[19]
- More likely to seek social support and emphasize the positive aspects of a stressful situation[20]
- Less likely to die over 30 years of follow-up[21]

In an interesting series of studies, psychologists Barbara Fredrickson, PhD, of the University of Michigan, and Robert Levenson, PhD, of the University of California, Berkeley, were looking for the biological mechanisms that make positive emotions health promoting.[22] In one study, subjects were shown a video that elicited fear, followed by films designed to elicit either neutrality/sadness or contentment/amusement. Everyone experienced increases in heart rate and blood pressure during the scary movie, but people who watched the positive, contentment/amusement film afterward experienced a much more rapid recovery from those responses, compared with those who watched the neutral/sad video.

In a second study, subjects watched a video that elicited sadness. Those who were observed to smile spontaneously during the film showed a more rapid return of blood pressure and heart rate to resting levels than subjects who didn't smile.

In another study, University of Pittsburgh psychologist Thomas Kamarck, PhD, took an experience that terrifies many of us—public speaking—and showed in a laboratory reenactment that having a friend sitting nearby reduces blood pressure and heart rate surges during this stressful task.[23]

The evidence is clear: The positive attitude and social support enjoyed by people in control of their emotions protects them against the fight-or-flight responses they would normally experience with negative emotions.

Enter Emotional Intelligence

Another trend in current psychology that meshes well with our research is the area of emotional intelligence. As formulated by psychologists Peter Salovey, PhD, of Yale, and Jack Mayer, PhD, of the University of New Hampshire[24]—and popularized in the writings of Daniel Goleman, PhD[25]—the concept refers to the intelligent use of emotions to guide behavior and thinking, thereby increasing personal effectiveness. Emotional intelligence as presented by Dr. Goleman consists of five main skills or competencies.

- *Self-awareness:* awareness of emotions and accurate self-assessment
- *Self-regulation:* the ability to control emotions and impulses, flexibility in handling change, and the ability to innovate
- *Motivation:* a high need to achieve and initiate; optimism (which links emotional intelligence with positive psychology)
- *Empathy:* the ability to tune in to emotional states of other people, increased altruism, the ability to understand and develop relationships, and a willingness to meet others' needs
- *Social skills:* Persuasiveness, conflict management, and leadership

People with high levels of emotional intelligence are more successful in a wide range of pursuits, including not only their relationships with important people in their lives but also their ability to move quickly up the corporate ladder. When we looked at the factors that make up emotional intelligence, it quickly became evident to us that our training program was also well tailored to increase emotional intelligence.

Finding the Flow

Another concept relevant to our research and this program is "flow," defined by University of Chicago psychologist Mihaly Csikszentmihalyi,

PhD, as an intensely rewarding state of deep absorption. Flow is achieved when a person's perceptions of a challenging situation and his ability to handle that situation are equally balanced. When the perceived challenge greatly exceeds the necessary skill level, or the person's skills exceed the demands of the challenge, apathy and boredom set in.[26] By providing skills that enable people to cope successfully with more stressful situations, our program should enhance the ability to experience flow in situations that previously would have been overwhelming.

The Great Effects of Self-Efficacy

The concept of self-efficacy, as developed by Stanford University psychologist Albert Bandura, PhD, is also relevant to our work. It involves the belief that a person is competent to perform at reasonable levels in a given situation—a personal judgment based on past experiences of success.[27] Enhanced self-efficacy increases your commitment to achieving higher goals for yourself, linking it to the motivation component of emotional intelligence.

By enhancing your ability and competence to handle difficult situations, our 8-week program should increase your sense of self-efficacy, which will lead to increased motivation and optimism.

As you can see, our program draws upon many areas of research. All of these fields, along with our experiences, combine to document the potential benefits of being in control. Solid epidemiological studies that follow people over time have found that the combination of less bad stuff (hostility, depression, and job stress) and more good stuff (optimism, positive emotions, and supportive social ties) reduces your risk of getting sick and your risk of suffering serious complications if major illness is present. The benefits also include better health habits. We can thank very elegant laboratory studies for helping identify the mechanism that's probably responsible for those benefits—a shorter, smaller fight-or-flight response when stressed. The likely result of achieving this change? A longer, healthier, happier life.

DO YOU BOUNCE BACK?

Although Sarah briefly felt depressed 3 weeks after her surgery, the feelings were transitory. Her emerging skills helped her to draw upon a number of positive factors in her situation. First, she was able to benefit from the considerable support available from both Hal and her daughters. They made it very clear, in their own ways, just how much they cared for Sarah. Second, she clearly took a positive, optimistic approach to her recovery—she reached out to her family. Third, she took constructive charge of her personal time by resigning her job, going to rehab, and attending a support group.

Sarah's enhanced ability to look on the bright side, even when things seemed dark—to reach down, grab those bootstraps, lift herself up, and do what she needed to do to make things better—was vital to her survival.

Do you handle adversity with the same sort of optimistic, positive, can-do attitude that began to emerge in Sarah during the months following her heart attack and bypass surgery? Do you have family members or friends who will rally around, help you cope, and listen sympathetically when bad things happen? Do you *let* them provide this support by welcoming it instead of shutting them out?

If you already look on the brighter side even when the pathway is dark, consider yourself fortunate. Like Sarah, you can harness these strengths to help you learn to be in control. If looking on the bright side seems challenging, you'll want to pay close attention to Weeks 6 through 8 of the program.

WHERE IT ALL BEGINS

When Sarah thought back to her childhood, she had mixed feelings. She had never been spanked or denied material things; she always had nicer clothes than her friends. Nevertheless, while she was growing up, her father was more likely to criticize than to praise. If she missed a single note at a piano recital, that was what she heard about—nothing about the rest of the piece that everyone else told her she had played with skill and feeling. For every compliment her father gave, there seemed to be at least one critical remark.

Sarah's mother seemed unable to counter her father's negativity, perhaps because she received her share of negative comments from him, too. While protective, her mother was constantly on guard, warning Sarah not to upset her father. As Sarah entered her teen years, whenever she sang "Home on the Range," she modified one of the refrains: ". . . where seldom is heard an encouraging word . . ."

The skies were not "cloudy all day" in every aspect of Sarah's life, however, thanks to her maternal grandparents. Her grandmother was a warm, doting person. In her eyes, Sarah could do no wrong, so visits with her grandparents were almost the direct opposite of Sarah's experience at home. During the month or so that she spent there every summer between the ages of 8 and 12, she heard nothing but praise: Her hair was so silky. Her piano playing was beautiful—would she play when company came? Her grandmother often gushed to her friends, "We love to have Sarah. She's such a delight!"

These contrasting experiences had an impact as Sarah grew up. On the one hand, she learned to be wary of others; on the other, she believed at some level that she was a capable person, thanks to her grandparents' positive messages.

A growing body of scientific evidence documents the impact of your childhood environment and your genes on your adult ways of coping. When Redford and several other leading behavioral medicine researchers began to see a clustering of psychosocial risk factors, biological markers of stress, and risky health behaviors in the same individuals and groups, they turned their attention to childhood. There's no doubt that the development of health-damaging characteristics is set in motion there. Extreme levels of abuse and neglect have long been known to be significantly harmful. Violence, depression, and medical illnesses are observed far more often in people who were subjected to severe stresses as children.[28] But what about lower levels of childhood stress—adversity within the "normal" range?

Some years ago, one of Redford's graduate students, Linda Luecken, wanted to test an idea. She thought that young adults who had experienced the death of a parent during childhood would show adverse effects in both their psychological and biological characteristics. While the death of a parent is surely very traumatic for any child, it's not as damaging as the more extensive active abuse and neglect that produce extreme adult maladjustments. Luecken's study provided the opportunity to see what a less severe, but still serious, level of adversity in childhood can do to affect adults.

In a battery of psychological tests, young adults who had lost one parent scored higher for depression and hostility than those who hadn't had such a loss, suggesting that they possessed less control of their negative emotions. The loss group also scored lower on a measure of social support, suggesting lower levels of skills that would foster more positive supportive relationships.

Luecken also had another good idea: She wanted to see if the impact of loss on the people in her study might differ depending on what kind of family relationships they experienced following the loss, particularly with the surviving parent. Those who reported less-positive family environments following a parent's death showed higher depression and lower social support levels. This group's depression scores were high enough to be considered indicative of a clinically significant level of depression. As shown in the graph on page 22, people who had lost a parent but reported positive family environments during the following years actually scored *lower* for depression than even the subjects in the non-loss group, in whom family environment didn't have much effect on depression.[29]

Luecken also evaluated some biological markers of stress. She found that the loss group had higher blood pressure, both at rest and when challenged to talk about a stressful situation. They also showed greater increases in levels of the stress hormone cortisol in their saliva following the interview. Just as with depression, however, it was only those who reported more

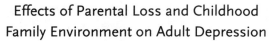

Effects of Parental Loss and Childhood Family Environment on Adult Depression

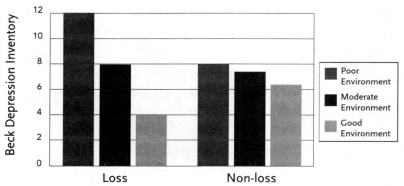

negative family environments who showed cortisol increases; among the loss subjects who reported good family environments, cortisol levels were similar to those in the non-loss group.[30]

So there's some bad news: The loss of a parent during childhood can have negative effects in adulthood. But there's also some good news: Even tragic childhood experiences may lead to a balanced and in-control adulthood if there were people in the child's life to offer positive, caring support. The end result can be even greater resilience, perhaps because of enduring the adversity, having help to overcome it, and becoming stronger.

But what about more ordinary kinds of difficulty, such as parents who get divorced, don't pay attention to how their child is doing in school, have problems with substance abuse, or tend to be more critical than encouraging? Luecken's student, Amy Kraft, studied adult children of divorce. Compared to adults from intact families, previous research had shown their health is worse. But in Kraft's study, the amount of time their fathers spent with them after the divorce directly affected their levels of the stress hormone cortisol. The more time fathers spent with their children after the divorce, the less these adult children responded to a stressful situation. And when adult children with highly involved fathers were looked at as a group, those from divorced families had even lower cortisol responses than those from intact families.[31]

The truth is, even lesser degrees of adversity can impair the development of healthy coping skills. For example:

- Children who live in unsafe neighborhoods or whose parents don't bother to know how they're doing in school are more likely to become obese.[32]

- Children who hear fewer positive communications from their parents between birth and 3 years of age have lower verbal IQ scores when tested 5 to 6 years later.[33]

- Children with parents who give few positive communications during discussion of a conflict topic, like keeping a room neat, become increasingly hostile as they become older.[34]

IT'S IN YOUR GENES, TOO

It's not only nurture (the childhood environment we experience) but also nature (the genes we inherit from our parents) that contributes to our ability to keep our lives in control. Perhaps the clearest demonstration comes from research on newborns conducted by Harvard psychologist Jerome Kagan, PhD.

Dr. Kagan's research shows that from birth, well before any environmental influences are exerted, about 10 percent of babies are shy. They appear to experience such strong negative emotions when confronted with new people and situations that they prefer to withdraw—a characteristic that could make it harder for them to gain social support later in life. Another 10 percent of babies are outgoing, exploring every nook and cranny with little hesitation. Of course, that leaves 80 percent of us more or less in the middle, where the way we're treated by our parents can push us toward either the shy or outgoing end of the continuum.

Despite the hardwired nature of this tendency toward shyness, Dr. Kagan's research shows that it's not beyond the influence of nurture, in the form of parents' behavior. Shy children with supportive mothers are able to decrease their bashfulness. Such mothers are patient and gentle in drawing them out, letting them move at their own pace but always encouraging them. And while children who are born shy will never be as outgoing as kids who are naturally extroverted, they can grow up to be much less bashful.[35]

Similarly, researchers have long known that boys who suffer extreme abuse are more likely to have behavior problems in adulthood, ranging from antisocial conduct and personality disorders all the way to criminal acts of violence. But that's not the whole story. A study reported in the journal *Science* shows that genes can still make a difference, for good or ill, in how a very stressful childhood environment can affect an adult. The gene in question is another that's involved in regulating the neurotransmitter serotonin. It makes an enzyme called monoamine oxidase A (MAOA), which is responsible for breaking down serotonin into an inactive form. As you may recall, low levels of serotonin have been associated with high levels of aggression and violence. Thus, there's good reason to think that the MAOA gene may influence violent tendencies by affecting serotonin levels in the brain.

Like all genes, the MAOA gene comes in slightly different forms, one of which makes more of the MAOA enzyme than another, less active form. Some of the men in the *Science* study had been subjected to severe abuse during childhood, which would be expected to increase their likelihood of violent behavior. Compared with men who hadn't been abused, those who experienced severe abuse were five to six times more likely to have been convicted of violent offenses, but only if they had the less active form of the MAOA gene.[36]

When it comes to extreme behaviors, both nurture and nature are involved in determining the degree of sensitivity to the effects of extremely adverse environments. Most people are not subjected to such extreme conditions during childhood, but as we noted earlier, more normal levels of adversity can also affect adult potential. All of these factors have a hand in your personality and how you respond to the world around you.

DID YOU HAVE A SUPPORTIVE CHILDHOOD?

As you look back, do you remember having the kind of positive, supportive childhood experiences that Sarah knew during those wonderful summer sojourns at her grandparents' house? Do you recall less positive, more critical relationships such as she had at home? Or, like most of us, do you see a mix of both types? After you take the Self-Assessment Quiz in Chapter 2, think about your childhood experiences and how they may have influenced your score.

If you recall mainly positive, supportive people in your childhood environment, chances are your score will be rather high. If your childhood experiences were more mixed, or even mainly negative, you probably will score lower. If that's the case, however, you are not locked in at that level! We've described how even children who endured the loss of a parent or were born incredibly shy can overcome these factors with some patient encouragement. Now you have the opportunity to show yourself that kind of loving support. The 8-week plan detailed in Part 2 was designed in part to help us and others redress some of the inequities of our youth, and they can work for you, too. It's never too late.

MOVING TOWARD CONTROL

When Hal and Sarah thought she was back on her feet again, they took the trip to the Caribbean that they had postponed following her heart attack. They went too soon, however, and Sarah experienced disturbing symptoms that laid her low as soon as they arrived. Her chest hurt, she became tired easily, and she experienced shortness of breath. Instead of lying on the beach, she spent 4 days in the local hospital. They returned home as soon as the doctors cleared her to travel.

The following fall, they decided to forgo their usual trip to Florida. Instead, they headed for the Southwest, checking out the lifestyle in that part of the country and visiting several golf resorts. Once back in their wintry northern metropolis, they couldn't stop talking about how happy they had been on the trip. The more they thought about it, the more they liked the idea of retiring, moving to Arizona, and settling in one of the upscale golf communities they had visited. They were especially attracted to one close to Tucson, with its educational and cultural resources.

Hal took an early retirement package from his company and quickly found a consulting job in Tucson. He moved that January, while Sarah stayed north until their house was sold. Originally, they had planned to stay in Hal's apartment while they built a house in the club community they liked best, but it didn't take them long to realize that they didn't need to take on all the hassles of building. They bought a nice house in the community that had just come on the market. Problem solved.

This decision reflected Sarah's new resolve to "keep it simple." (When she had announced this resolution to her friends back home, they had laughed, knowing how Sarah usually took the complicated route.) Once she and Hal had relocated, Sarah took a number of steps to establish a circle of friends in Arizona. She went through cardiac rehab again at the heart center at a university hospital, connecting with another group of folks who were working hard to enhance their recovery from heart disease. She even helped start a book club.

She also volunteered a few afternoons each week at the heart center, sharing her experiences with others who were scheduled for heart surgery. This helped Sarah keep her own spirits up, as well as those of the patients she talked with. She recalled one fairly young woman with heart disease whose surgery was unsuccessful and who died shortly after going home. The woman's family sent a letter to the heart center, noting that Sarah's attention had meant a lot. "You were a comfort to her, and she looked forward to your visits," they wrote.

It hasn't always been smooth sailing for her, though. She currently has chronic pain in both legs, which doctors tell her is due to nerve degeneration, and although *medication helps, she can't stand for long periods. She hasn't let her infirmities get her down, however; she's taken up painting and goes to a class three times a week. Painting distracts her, and the pain seems less intense. "I work hard at having a positive attitude," she says.*

Sarah continues to struggle to keep her distrust of others and frequent feelings of annoyance at bay. She now checks out initial impressions against objective information and evaluates options. Sometimes, she takes action; other times, she has learned to chill out.

From the time of her heart attack, Sarah went through all the stages of grieving, including anger, over the loss of her prior disease-free life. She attended a few weekend retreats to help her through the process. As she put it, though, she has "finally gotten to acceptance."

It took a heart attack, time, and hard work to get her moving, but Sarah is far more in control today than she was on that inauspicious New Year's Day several years ago. Despite her continuing medical problems, she moves toward the future confidently, developing skills that will help her cope—and feel good about herself in the process.

Sarah didn't magically transform herself overnight during this journey. She sought out experiences—the weekend retreats, the support groups—that collectively helped her to be proactive and emphasize the positive. All of this work helped her make this important, life-affirming transition. In the process, she's improved her marriage, her relationship with her children, and her ability to make friends and surround herself with people who support her. She's also probably saved her own life a dozen times over. While it may have taken some time, Sarah is now enjoying herself more.

As we said earlier, people who don't have a sense of control over their lives experience, on average, more anger, depression, and social isolation—and less social interaction, happiness, self-esteem, and self-efficacy. As a result, they also experience, on average, more health problems. And they tend to not live as long.

The good news is that whatever your starting point, it is possible to gain control of your life. When you do, your health and well-being are likely to improve quickly and dramatically. And there's evidence to prove it.

STUDIES SHOW IT'S POSSIBLE TO CONTROL HOW YOU REACT TO STRESS

Beginning in the early 1980s, several randomized clinical trials of behavioral strategies (the precursors of our 8-week program) targeted certain psychological and social risk factors in people with heart disease or cancer. By chance assignment, some subjects were taught the strategies, while others were put in a control group and didn't learn the strategies. Randomized clinical trials are considered the gold standard when it comes to proving that new treatments—whether new drugs or behavioral approaches—are effective in treating or preventing disease. These early studies found some amazing results.

- People with malignant melanoma (a type of skin cancer) who received training in coping skills to handle stress slashed their recurrence rate by 50 percent and their death rate by an astonishing 70 percent.[37]

- Heart attack patients who received training that reduced both hostility and depression cut their risk of recurring heart attacks or death in half.[38]

- Other heart patients who were trained to use coping skills to reduce stress cut their risk of having subsequent heart attacks or needing bypass surgery or angioplasty by more than 50 percent.[39]

One of our corporate clients found that training decreased bad stuff, such as depression and hostility, and increased good stuff, such as social support and self-esteem, among employees. These results were obtained in what might be described as "open label trials" of our program (in other words, there was no randomized control group). Now there have been two carefully conducted randomized clinical trials of patients with heart disease that document these benefits more rigorously.

In the first, psychologist Karina Davidson, PhD, and her student Yori Gidron at Dalhousie University in Halifax, Nova Scotia, randomly assigned heart attack patients to groups that received either the usual care or training to reduce hostility, which was based on an earlier version of our 8-week program. At the end of eight training sessions, those in the hostility-reduction group showed significant decreases in both hostility and blood pressure compared with those who received the usual care. More important, when the researchers followed up with the patients after 2 months, they found that both hostility and blood pressure levels had decreased even further in those receiving hostility-reduction training, while levels had drifted up slightly in those receiving the usual care.[40] After 6 months, those who had received hostility-reduction training had been hospitalized again for an average of only about ½ day, compared with 2.5 days for the usual-care group.

A more recent randomized clinical trial was conducted by psychologist George Bishop, PhD, at the National University of Singapore and the National Heart Centre there. In that study, people who had undergone coronary bypass surgery were randomly assigned to either the usual care or to our coping skills workshop. Because we trained Dr. Bishop and his colleagues to deliver the workshop, the training was provided to the patients in Singapore just as it is in the United States, with some adaptations for Far Eastern culture. (For example, instead of practicing assertion toward someone who has distressed you, you would have a friend or relative act as an intermediary, thereby ensuring that no one would lose face.)

As first presented at the Annual Scientific Sessions of the American Heart Association in Chicago in November 2002, Dr. Bishop's study both confirmed and extended the results obtained by Dr. Davidson and Gidron. When tested 3 months after the workshops were completed, the patients who received our training were better off on several fronts than those who received the usual care. For example:

- They experienced less psychosocial bad stuff: lower scores on depression (a 60 percent decrease), anger (18 percent), and perceived stress (18 percent).

- They experienced less biological bad stuff: lower resting heart rate (a 9 percent decrease) and reduced reactivity of blood pressure (56 percent) and heart rate (65 percent) when angered.

- They experienced more psychosocial good stuff: higher scores for satisfaction with social support (a 14 percent increase) and satisfaction with life (13 percent).[41]

These results provide direct evidence that training in coping skills can really change not only people's ability to improve their emotional lives but also their physical prognoses and prospects for future health. In addition, the results also help us see how, in many ways, we've completed an odyssey that mirrors Sarah's. Prior to her heart attack, she was preoccupied with the bad stuff—overly controlling, stressed by work and family, not getting as much support as she needed. But following her heart attack, she tried to simplify things. She cut out the bad stuff and increased the good stuff by connecting with her family, making new friends, and looking after herself.

More than a decade ago, we began with a primary concern to understand how bad stuff made people sick and to develop a training program to ameliorate those effects. We learned during these years, however, that we need to show people more than just how to reduce the bad stuff; we need to teach skills that increase the good stuff as well. Our odyssey mirrored not only Sarah's but also a trend in American psychology that increasingly recognizes the need to devote more attention to enhancing positive attributes while continuing to work on ways to reduce negative factors. *In Control* is the *combination* of more good stuff and less bad stuff.

NOW IT'S YOUR TURN

You don't need to wait for a heart attack or other major illness or life-changing event to start your journey. You probably won't even take as long as Sarah did to gain control of your life. She had to find her way slowly, on her own, and make her changes by trial and error; you can get started right now by following the 8-week program in Part 2.

But first, turn to Chapter 2 and take the Self-Assessment Quiz. You may find that you score in the low or medium range, but you know now that your initial score is just the beginning. You know from reading about Sarah's experience and the scientific evidence that it's possible to improve your coping skills, and that doing so will improve both your emotional well-being and, possibly, your physical health. And that's just the beginning! Remember the other proven benefits enjoyed by those who have undergone this type of training.

- Less hostility and anger
- Less anxiety
- Healthier heart rate and blood pressure, both at rest and when experiencing negative emotions (such as anger)
- More support from friends and loved ones
- Greater satisfaction with life

While more research remains to be done to determine the exact degree of protection provided by training, everything we know points to the fact that people in control will live longer and, equally important, live *better*. Don't waste another moment—it's time to join the winner's circle!

CHAPTER 2

ARE YOU IN CONTROL?

Now you've read the evidence that people with a sense of control live happier, healthier, longer lives. When presented with the evidence that having a sense of control leads to happier, healthier, and longer lives, people often ask next, "Am I in control?" If they take the Self-Assessment Quiz or hear some feedback that suggests the answer is no, the inevitable second question is, "Why aren't I in control?" This quiz will help with both answers.

We developed and tested the quiz in an attempt to measure each of the skills necessary to having a sense of control. Once we'd perfected it, we added it to a battery of tests in an ongoing study to measure the effectiveness of coping skills training.

The results were impressive: The quiz strongly correlated with other nationally standardized tests for long- and short-term anxiety, depression, hostility, perceived stress, and social support. We saw that, on average, the lower a person's skill level, the higher his levels of anxiety, depression, hostility, and perceived stress. We also found that people's social support scores were lower when their skills were lower and higher when their skills were higher. In sum, the quiz mirrors those psychosocial factors that predict increased risk of serious health problems. Pleased with these results, we presented these findings at the 2003 annual meeting of the Society for Behavioral Medicine in Salt Lake City.[1]

The primary objective of the quiz is to get a reading on where you stand now. We've found it can be helpful—and gratifying—to get an idea of where you stand *before* starting the 8-week program, then take the test again to see if you've improved your scores. You should interpret your scores as general tendencies rather than precise descriptions.

Based on what you learned in the preceding chapter, you may or may not be happy with your scores—but don't fret! The solution lies in Part 2.

TAKING THE SELF-ASSESSMENT QUIZ

First, find a notebook or journal to keep track of all the work you'll be doing in the 8-week program. Shoot for at least 100 pages, either lined or unlined. (A small spiral-bound notebook is usually handiest, since you can fit it into your bag or pocket for use in critical moments.) On the first page, write the numbers 1 through 30 on each line.

Next, answer each question in the quiz by circling the number that best represents your actions or feelings—from 1, meaning never, to 5, meaning always. Since your first answers are usually the most accurate, answer as quickly as you can and avoid the temptation to look for the most socially desirable answers. No one else needs to know your scores, so there's no reason to fudge.

When you're finished, write these numbers in your notebook. Then look at the scoring instructions on page 35 and calculate your totals for each skill as well as your total score. In a month or two, you'll probably want to re-take the quiz to see how far you've progressed.

NEVER		SOMETIMES		ALWAYS

1. I know right away when I'm angry.

1	2	3	4	5

2. If it's bad weather on my day off, I get over it quickly.

1	2	3	4	5

NEVER   SOMETIMES   ALWAYS

3. My stress level is low.

  1   2   3   4   5

4. If stuck without a ride, I find a way of getting where I want to go.

  1   2   3   4   5

5. When the waiter brings the wrong dish, I ask for a replacement.

  1   2   3   4   5

6. I'm good at saying no.

  1   2   3   4   5

7. I can tell people what I'm feeling.

  1   2   3   4   5

8. In conversations, I listen about half the time.

  1   2   3   4   5

9. On airplanes, parents of crying toddlers don't bother me.

  1   2   3   4   5

10. I look for things to praise in others.

  1   2   3   4   5

11. I know right away when I'm sad.

  1   2   3   4   5

12. Traffic jams don't bother me for very long.

  1   2   3   4   5

13. In a close game, I quickly get over an unfair call by the referee.

  1   2   3   4   5

14. When I have a problem, I ask others for ideas.

  1   2   3   4   5

15. I ask for a change when the car radio is tuned to a station I don't like.

  1   2   3   4   5

16. I keep the number of tasks I take on to a manageable level.

  1   2   3   4   5

17. In disagreements, I focus on specific situations, not general trends.

  1   2   3   4   5

NEVER	SOMETIMES	ALWAYS

18. I avoid giving advice unless asked.

    1   2   3   4   5

19. I'm okay with people with driving styles different from mine.

    1   2   3   4   5

20. Most of my close relationships go well.

    1   2   3   4   5

21. I'm aware of my feelings.

    1   2   3   4   5

22. In bad situations, I can be counted on to be effective.

    1   2   3   4   5

23. When returning home after a tough day, I put it aside.

    1   2   3   4   5

24. I'm good at problem solving.

    1   2   3   4   5

25. When interrupted, I manage to continue speaking.

    1   2   3   4   5

26. My rewards at work are fair.

    1   2   3   4   5

27. I hold up my side of a conversation.

    1   2   3   4   5

28. In disagreements, I realize I could be wrong.

    1   2   3   4   5

29. I can accept as okay people with politics different from mine.

    1   2   3   4   5

30. When my significant other mispronounces a word, I say nothing.

    1   2   3   4   5

CALCULATING YOUR SCORE

Now that you've taken the quiz, you can determine your profile on the 10 skills that determine your degree of control. Copy the numbers you circled for each question into your notebook, then refer to the notebook as you fill in the section below.

Awareness
How aware are you of your feelings? (Skill 1)

    1.   _____

    11.   _____

    21.   _____

    Total _____

Evaluation
How often do you think situations through before reacting? (Skill 2)

    2.   _____

    12.   _____

    22.   _____

    Total _____

Deflection
Can you get over negative thoughts and/or feelings you don't want to have? (Skill 3)

    3.   _____

    13.   _____

    23.   _____

    Total _____

Solving problems
Are you good at solving problems? (Skill 4)

    4.   _____

    14.   _____

    24.   _____

    Total _____

Standing up for yourself

Do you ask for what you need and want? (Skill 5)

5. _____
15. _____
25. _____
Total _____

Are you self-protective? (Skill 6)

6. _____
16. _____
26. _____
Total _____

Communicating effectively

Do you speak in ways that make others likely to listen? (Skill 7)

7. _____
17. _____
27. _____
Total _____

Do you listen effectively? (Skill 8)

8. _____
18. _____
28. _____
Total _____

Understanding others

Do you understand others? (Skill 9)

9. _____
19. _____
29. _____
Total _____

Embodying positive values

Is your emphasis positive? (Skill 10)

10. _____

20. _____

30. _____

Total _____

Total score: _____ (sum of all scores)

INTERPRETING YOUR SCORE

You now have some data that's very helpful in determining your profile. The totals for each of the 10 sections are your individual scores, and the final total is your overall score. (In general, the higher your total score, the lower you're likely to score on negative health-damaging factors such as depression, anxiety, hostility, and your perception of stress, and the higher you're likely to score on positive health-promoting factors such as social support.) Here's what your overall score means.

If your score was 30: At this point, you essentially are almost never in control. Things have to change for you, and fast, if you want to improve your relationships and reduce your health risks. Chances are, you are probably dissatisfied and looking for some major changes. Luckily, you have the program that can help you right in your hands.

If your score was 31–60: Unfortunately, you are rarely in control. You may have a handle on one or two skills, but they are being overshadowed by your behavior in other facets of your life. Your best strategy is to focus on those traits in which you scored the lowest; those are the areas in your life where you're likely to see the biggest changes.

If your score was 61–90: You are sometimes in control. Perhaps you're where you want to be in some areas but not others, or your scores may be rather evenly distributed. You need to decide if there are areas you would like to improve. Part 2 will give you insights and strategies on how to improve the specific skills you need to focus on.

If your score was 91–120: You are often in control. You're probably living a very good life right now, but you may have a few challenge areas that you'd like to address. The quiz can help show you those areas that may be keeping you from leading your life in the best way possible. With some gentle exploration, you may find that the quality of your relationships and your motivation to succeed and do good work will only improve after following the 8-week program.

If your score was 121–150: You are almost always in control. Congratulations! You're probably enjoying a very rich life, packed with fulfilling friendships and interesting, gratifying pursuits. You've learned to master your emotions, and you're able to manage your environment to create better outcomes for everyone in your life. To that end, perhaps you'd like to brush up on the skills that brought you to the place you are now so you can help a friend, child, or other loved one adopt the same habits.

EVALUATING YOUR PROFILE

Next, look at your scores for each of the skills. A score of 3 indicates that you never use a particular skill, 9 shows that you sometimes do, and 15 indicates that you always use it. People's results vary widely. Here are some of the patterns we commonly see.

Weeks 1–5: These weeks cover how well you handle stressful situations. If you are a stuffer (low on Skill 1), there's a good chance that you also seldom ask for what you want or don't like to say no when you really need to (low on the skills in Skill 5 and 6). You may also tend to let bad feelings fester (low on Skill 3).

If you tend to act before thinking (low on Skill 2), you may not be good at chilling out (low on Skill 3). You also may benefit from better problem-solving ability (Skill 4), asking for what you want in a way that doesn't offend others (Skill 5) and saying no (Skill 6).

Weeks 6–8: Here the focus is on relationships. Many of us are either effective speakers or good listeners (Skills 7 and 8). To be a good communicator, you need to be both. Most people who find listening challenging also aren't good at reading others (Skill 9).

Your score for Skill 10 provides an overview of your general attitudes toward your life and the people in it. Your score here is probably similar to the average of your scores on the others. If you do score higher on the other skills than on this one, you should know that a simple strategy can help you shift your thinking and increase your ability to see the world—and your life—from a more positive perspective.

YOUR STRATEGY

Now, working with the information from your scores, you can develop a strategy. How would you sum up your profile at this point?

Areas I'm satisfied with:

_____

_____

_____

_____

Areas I'd like to focus on:

_____

_____

_____

_____

Once you've finished the 8-week program, you can settle in to work on your specific skills with more focus. It's up to you to decide whether you're satisfied with your current score for each area. Keep these scores in your notebook, but try to forget about the quiz for the time being. It's just a snapshot of where you are right now, not a permanent image. Continue thinking about the big picture.

Once you've been working with the skills for a while, turn to the Appendix and get ready to take the same quiz again to see if your scores have changed. (Before filling in the answers, photocopy the quiz so you can take it again later.) Most likely, you'll find that they have, since the training will still be fresh in your mind. Six months later, repeat the quiz. Are you still on track? You may notice that you're slipping a bit, which sometimes happens. Progress, not perfection, is the goal. Repeat the entire evaluation to determine your challenge areas, which may have changed in the intervening months, and update your strategy.

You'll probably find that the skills you've acquired are working so well that you'll keep using them. We studied the effects of our training on employees at a large corporation. Two weeks after training, participants had reduced their levels of depression, anger, and stress. Six months later, these levels were down even further. If you will continue to practice, your levels will likely continue to decline.

From the very beginning, using the skills will help to influence your friends, colleagues, and family—everyone in your life. That's the ultimate benefit of the process: Each step you take, each time you take it, helps create the kind of healthy, supportive, happy environment in which it becomes easier and easier to be in control.

Now it's time to begin learning the process. Turn to Week 1: Recognize Your Emotions (see page 45).

PART ②

GAINING CONTROL

CHAPTER 3

WEEK 1: RECOGNIZE YOUR EMOTIONS

This week, you'll learn to use awareness of your feelings as a wakeup call. Your body will tell you, "Pay attention! Observe what is happening right here, right now!" Mindfulness will help you key into important situations that might otherwise be ignored or swept under the rug. This awareness is the foundation skill of the 8-week program.

When Merrison Andrews was a 23-year-old bride living in Ohio, she was often referred to as voluptuous. She looked great in a sweater and jeans. Curvy and tall, with wavy red hair, she frequently got second glances. But Merrison's personality didn't match her hair: She seldom saw red or made waves.

During the early years of her marriage, Merrison focused primarily on community activities. In addition to her job as a financial specialist, she liked to direct projects for nonprofit groups and her church.

As the years passed, she experienced some of the crises that might be expected for a woman of her age and situation. Before she and her husband had their baby, though, she envisioned their new addition would be a spark that could add "zip" to their marriage. She quit her job near the end of her pregnancy so she could devote all of her time to her family. When the baby was born, however, she came to the same realization as many other new mothers: That "zip" might actually be on hold for a long time, since now she and her husband had less time and energy for each other. The baby seemed to absorb all the moments the two had previously shared alone. To compound matters, her husband got a promotion that required him to travel much more often. With her new daughter to care for, Merrison cut back on outside activities and seldom spent time with friends.

At that time, Merrison couldn't identify exactly what was wrong. Hadn't she gotten just what she wanted: the model husband, a comfortable and attractive home, the baby she had longed for? Yet something felt slightly "off."

Merrison tried to make staying at home with the baby as enjoyable as possible. One of the things that really worked was fixing treats, and baking made the house smell wonderful. In the first few months after her daughter was born, while the baby napped, Merrison spent the mornings in the kitchen preparing goodies, then sampling: Toll House cookies, brownies, homemade peach ice cream. Her friends began to call her "Ohio's own three-star chef." The pregnancy weight wasn't coming off, but Merrison decided not to worry about it right then. She would work on shedding the pounds when her energy and spirits returned to their pre-pregnancy levels. For now, she'd concentrate on being a mom.

Three years later, those 30 pounds were still there, and they began to really bother her. After her husband made a comment about her weight, she decided it was time to act. She began to exercise and joined a local support group for people who were trying to slim down.

Merrison had lost 10 pounds and was feeling really good about herself when her husband was offered another promotion—but this one was different. If he took the new job, the family would have to relocate to Chile for a few years. She and her husband sat down to discuss it, but in the back of her mind, she knew the decision was already made. Leaving the friends she'd made in her weight-loss group would be hard, but the reality was, her husband's salary would stretch much further in Chile. They could afford to hire household help. Maybe the whole family would even pick up Spanish. After numerous discussions, they decided to go, and Merrison was determined to make the best of it.

In Chile, the family enjoyed a standard of living far beyond what they'd known in the United States, but again, something felt vaguely wrong. Within the first

6 months after moving, Merrison regained the 10 pounds she'd lost. On a number of occasions each day, she could tell she was feeling "off." Rather than reacting, however, she just tried to ignore her malaise.

Eight months after moving to Chile, Merrison became pregnant. Once again, she became totally absorbed in caring for a newborn, but with the added responsibility of her young daughter. When she came up out of the fog 6 months after her son was born, Merrison realized she weighed 30 pounds more than before her second pregnancy—meaning she was now 60 pounds heavier than before her first one.

Still, she soldiered on, this time looking around for appealing hobbies or other activities to become engaged in, but she couldn't seem to find a good match for her interests. Merrison was delighted when her daughter began to pick up simple Spanish, even though her own attempts were less successful after almost 2 years in Chile.

Merrison Needed to Stop Suppressing Her Feelings

Several times each day, Merrison felt lonely, isolated, and ever more distant from her husband. When these feelings arose, she would fix a treat to make herself feel better, and it worked: She was temporarily soothed, and everything felt good and manageable. But each food fix lasted only a short time, and the cumulative effects of the treats were starting to have a long-term impact on her health and her sense of pride.

By turning to food for comfort, Merrison continued to avoid dealing with her problems head-on. Her first step had to be to acknowledge her feelings so she could deal directly with the situations causing them. That's why her first attempt at dieting had foundered: She had never admitted to herself how distressed she was by the isolation she felt after the birth of her daughter. This was a woman who had previously been very active, both at work and in her community. She was also no doubt dealing with the emotional upheaval of postpartum hormonal changes and the sleep deprivation that plagues most parents of young children.

Yet in her effort to maintain a happy home, Merrison squelched her feelings, which cut off any avenues of help to which she may have had access. Had she *admitted her feelings, she would have had many options. She could have asked her husband to relieve her more often, or hired a trusted babysitter so she could reestablish contact with her friends, or work on her beloved community projects. She could have connected with other young mothers in the community with whom she could plan some joint activities. Perhaps she could have strapped her daughter on her back and taken long walks through her neighborhood or along a nature trail. Or maybe she and her husband could have talked about ways to have some fun together despite the extra demands that had been brought on by his promotion.*

She had countless options that she didn't even consider because she didn't allow herself to acknowledge her negative feelings. Even when the family moved to Chile, where her options were somewhat more limited, Merrison could have explored a number of possibilities for enriching her life — if she had been willing to acknowledge that she was feeling distressed. Instead, she remained lonely, distraught, and emotionally hungry, so she ate.

Getting in touch with feelings isn't easy, especially for someone like Merrison, whom we call a stuffer. She'd probably learned to self-medicate with food long before her life hit a critical point. Some people may eat more during a life crisis because as children they associated eating with being rewarded. Perhaps their parents often said, "You've been so good today, here's a sweet." Other people may eat more to soothe themselves. Eating raises brain levels of the neurotransmitter serotonin, a chemical in the nervous system that reduces anxiety and induces a state of calm. Laboratory research on animals shows that during the act of eating, there is increased release of calming serotonin into a part of the brain that controls fight-or-flight behavior.[1]

No matter what the multiple origins of Merrison's overeating were, in addition to eating healthfully and exercising regularly, she needed to learn healthier coping skills. Practicing them would help her control her emotional eating — a pesky problem for many people.

For everyone, whether you have a weight problem or not, the first step to gaining control of your emotions and your life is to acknowledge your thoughts and especially your feelings.

DON'T STUFF IT

Most of us know generally when we're in a bad mood or something's "not right," but the key to lasting change is to get specific. Once you home in on the real reasons you feel that way, your possibilities expand. At first, though, it may be easier for you to acknowledge feelings if you realize their importance.

Realize that everyone has feelings. Unless you're trying to mask your feelings, your face normally expresses what's going on inside. Your brows knit in anger. Your mouth droops when you're sad. Your eyes open wide when you feel fear. Your lips curl up in happiness. Think about it: When you're disgusted with something, your face looks as if you just tasted something bitter.

Your face contains hundreds of muscles that react to the faintest internal cues. Experts can clearly read your feelings in many subtle variations by looking at your face. By examining many faces all around the world, these experts have determined that certain facial expressions—and therefore emotions—are universal (see "Everyone Has Emotions" on page 50). These expressions transcend language, culture, and ethnic origins; they are simply part and parcel of being human.

Yet sometimes, in efforts to keep the peace—or because of fear of what will happen if we actually admit, "Hey, I'm mad!"—we try to deny what we're feeling. No one, not even yourself, ever has the right to tell you that you aren't experiencing a particular feeling. Feelings just *are*—they're not a reflection of your character or a report card measuring how good a person you can claim to be. They're certainly not a prediction of your future. They just exist. What you do with these feelings is a different matter altogether, but your first step is to acknowledge that they simply have a right to be.

Realize that feelings deserve attention. Feelings tell you "Pay attention! Something important is happening right here, right now!"

Everyone Has Emotions

When times are tough, you may be tempted to think that you're the only one feeling the way you do, but you're only human—and we're (almost) all built with the same emotional wiring. Experts have found that we share many common feelings.[2]

UNIVERSAL FEELINGS

- Anger
- Sadness
- Fear
- Enjoyment
- Disgust

PROBABLY UNIVERSAL FEELINGS

- Contempt
- Surprise
- Interest

WIDESPREAD FEELINGS

- Love
- Shame

Sometimes feelings are positive. Maybe all that's required is to savor the moment. Take deep pleasure in that first strawberry of the season. Appreciate the sight and smell of the gardenia blossom, the freshly baked bread, the sleeping baby.

Other times, good feelings arise in response to the way you're being treated. If that's the case, consider thanking the person or at least calling attention to what's happening. Praise has the miraculous ability to increase the likelihood that such behavior will continue or at least be repeated at other times.

On the other hand, awareness of negative feelings can serve as a wake-up call that enables you to deal with situations on the spot. You can address small problems before they become too large. Let's look at an example.

You're in the second of a series of meetings about a project to which you've been assigned. Early on, you become aware of feeling bad. You pay attention and realize the reason you're feeling bad is that your colleague is taking all the credit for work you've done together. After the meeting, this awareness leads you to ask that person to acknowledge joint ownership from now on.

Now, if you weren't attuned to the origins of your feelings, you might go back to your desk in a funk or call a friend to complain about the meeting. You might even begin letting the project slip as a subconscious act of sabotage. Instead, the ultimate result of acknowledging your feelings is that you'll get the credit you deserve, and your energy will be freed to devote to doing your best on the project and getting even more accolades. You won't displace those bad feelings onto another person or situation later; you won't store up a whole series of unacknowledged resentments until something triggers an explosion and you find yourself frustrated and swearing, "I'll never work with X again!"

Awareness of negative feelings can help your marriage, too. Instead of letting little annoyances and grievances pile up, you and your spouse can discuss them and work to reach a compromise.

Let's say that you've realized you're grumpy most evenings once you finish cleaning up the kitchen and getting the children to bed. You've gotten into the habit of snapping at your partner and retiring to the TV. Tuning in to your own feelings may allow you to see that you're feeling resentful about shouldering both the cleanup and the bedtime tuck-ins. This awareness may lead to a request that results in sharing responsibilities. You would then become less grumpy and resentful—and you could even find that your sex life improves!

Such are the rewards of increasing awareness: fewer disheartening or cheerless episodes of frustration; lots more happiness.

Feelings need to be acknowledged at the moment they occur. Say a co-worker insults you, but you don't realize you're angry until that evening. It's too late to address the incident with your colleague — or at least doing so won't have the same impact as if you had discussed it on the spot. But before you realized you were upset by the earlier insult, you yelled at your partner about a completely unrelated matter. The displaced energy that had built up was dumped at the wrong time on the wrong person for the wrong reason.

Failing to take action at the moment an upsetting event occurs can result in a number of other problems as well. If you never call your co-worker on the way she treated you, you allow her to get away with such behavior, which reinforces the same kind of action in the future. As a result, she's more likely to behave the same way again. You've actually done her a disservice by not acknowledging your own feelings.

Ignoring your feelings can have additional negative consequences. Think of how much attention it takes to distract yourself from your feelings. In an effort to get rid of that free-floating general sense of disquiet, many people turn to alcohol, tobacco, caffeine, or other drugs; to overeating; or even to spirit-deadening activities such as shopping compulsively, playing never-ending computer games, watching TV obsessively, or gambling.

Feelings can fuel constructive actions as well as destructive ones. Feelings can be a powerful energy source and can spur you toward positive action. Were you ever in love, living far away from your beloved? Remember how wonderful it was to visit, despite the distance? Under other circumstances, the trip might have seemed tiresome, but not when you were going to see your sweetheart.

Sometimes, your feelings let you know you need to take action to prevent something bad from happening. If civil rights leaders hadn't acted on their righteous anger, Rosa Parks's grandchildren might still be sitting in the back of the bus. Jesus's acknowledgment of his own anger at the money-changers in the temple was what galvanized him to throw them out. Had the citizens of Love Canal, New York, not filed suits requesting relocation, they might still own homes situated on top of a poisonous dump.

Mismanaging feelings, however, can drive you to actions you later regret. Your daughter spills the lemonade. You have a flash of anger and, without thinking, immediately yell at her. Later, you wish you had reacted differently as your relationship will no doubt suffer some damage—but you were *so* annoyed!

Both overreacting and underreacting can be problematic. We've seen how not being in touch with your feelings can cause problems, but the opposite is also true. If you find yourself reacting quickly, if you're what we call a volatile or hot reactor, you probably have no trouble being aware of your feelings. Week 2 will offer you the tools to move from awareness to your most constructive response.

TUNE IN TO YOUR BODY

When you're in a fight or heated discussion, have you ever stopped and watched yourself? Your body has a lot to teach; it can help you realize what you're feeling, which is probably why we have the phrase "body language." Let's try a guided imagery exercise to help you tune in to how your body expresses your feelings.

First, identify a person about whom you have positive feelings (be sure not to choose someone you may have mixed feelings about). Write the person's name on a blank page in your notebook.

Next, identify a person about whom you have negative feelings (once again, be sure not to choose someone toward whom you have mixed feelings). Write that name on the next page of your notebook. You're now ready to begin the exercise.

1. Sit comfortably in a chair and put your feet flat on the floor. Read through the next paragraph, then look at the first name, close your eyes, and engage in the suggested imagery. When you're finished, let the image of the person fade, then open your eyes.

When you think of this special person you love or care about deeply, picture that person seated beside you. Notice the person's face and eye and hair color. What kinds of facial expressions are most typical? Notice what the person is wearing. How does the person smell?

2. Once you've opened your eyes, read the following questions and repeat the process (close your eyes, let your mind render the image from the preceding paragraph, let the image fade, and open your eyes). Are you aware of physical sensations? Pay close attention to your chest, abdomen, throat, and forehead. What emotions are you feeling? Do you have any thoughts?

3. Next, picture the person one more time and repeat the exercise.

When this image has faded, stretch or get up and walk around for a minute, then return to your chair. Now you're ready for the second guided imagery, focusing on the person with whom you have problems. Again, use the complete process.

1. Picture the difficult person seated beside you, closer than you would like. Notice the person's face and eye and hair color. What kind of facial expressions are most typical? Notice what the person is wearing. How does the person smell?

2. Open your eyes, take a deep breath, and begin. Are you aware of physical sensations? Pay close attention to your chest, abdomen, throat, and forehead. What emotions are you feeling? Do you have any thoughts?

3. Finally, picture the person again and repeat the exercise.

When this image has faded, stretch or get up and walk around for a minute.

Now, think about what you observed, in terms of both feelings and body sensations. How did the two experiences differ?

Once you've made this comparison, check the lists below. People who do the preceding exercises frequently mention these reactions. Did any of them match your experience?

The Positive Image	The Negative Image
• Relaxed chest	• Tight chest
• Deep, regular breathing	• Shallow breathing
• Relaxed facial muscles	• Clenched jaw
• Slight smile	• Downturned lips
• Relaxed hands and arms	• Furrowed brow
	• Tight muscles in hands and arms
	• Faster heartbeat

Recognizing these reactions is especially important if you react to unpleasant situations either strongly or hardly at all. We find this exercise helpful for people on either side of the reaction spectrum.

For "hot" reactors, who are quick to anger: The sensations you experienced when you pictured the person with whom you have difficulty is what happens inside your body day in and day out. Other changes were occurring as well. When you're angry:

- Your blood pressure rises
- Your levels of stress hormones go up
- Your blood is more likely to clot

- Your body doesn't process sugar well

- Your immune system doesn't fight off infections as easily

Think of it this way: Do you want to let a number of situations throughout the day—not only the important but the petty as well—have this much power? Wouldn't *you* rather remain in control?

For overly "cool" reactors, who stuff their feelings: Even using body awareness, cool reactors sometimes find it difficult to identify specific emotions. If this happens, try to identify a more general feeling, such as "I'm upset" or "I'm pleased." If you can't do that, try to put your experience somewhere along a simple spectrum from positive to negative, like this:

Negative feelings ◄———— X ————► **Positive feelings**

On the extreme positive end, for example, you might put the feeling you have after receiving a genuine compliment from your partner or a close friend; on the negative end, you might put the experience of what you feel when you don't receive credit for hard work on a project. Try to locate your feelings somewhere on this line, without judging their worth or acceptability. Remember, feelings just *are.*

Whether they're specific or general, your feelings can help you tune in to important situations right away. Instead of sleepwalking through a variety of experiences without letting them enter your consciousness, you need to truly feel each one. Not only does this add texture and meaning to everyday occurrences, it also provides the opportunity to expand positive experiences by reinforcing what's going on. If you don't know you're feeling good, how can you ever reinforce or duplicate the conditions that produced that feeling?

Acknowledging your feelings is truly the first step in taking control of your own life. Instead of passively absorbing what's happening to you or around you, you are in a position to make decisions that will give you command over your environment. By the nature of how you choose to react to those feelings, you can make the conditions stop or continue, intensify or diminish. But that power begins with being aware.

From now on, pay attention to your body. Do you experience sensations similar to the ones that arose during the two guided imageries? When you do, pay attention: Something important is happening!

KEEP A THOUGHTS AND FEELINGS LOG

We often refer to the skills you'll learn this week as the foundation of our program. Once you know how you feel about a situation, you can begin to formulate your response to it. In order to devise an appropriate, thoughtful response to any situation, though, you need accurate data—and part of amassing accurate data is good record-keeping.

In our workshops, we've discovered that it can be very difficult to recall the specifics of the moments in your life that provoke strong positive or negative thoughts and feelings. It can be especially hard to remember the objective facts about a given situation that would hold up in a court of law. And while you may be able to recall a general mood, your exact, immediate thoughts and feelings vaporize very quickly. That's why a log can be so helpful. Here are some of the benefits.

- Increased awareness of the objectively observable facts of a particular situation
- Increased awareness of your thoughts, which are your interpretation of those facts
- Increased awareness of feelings
- Increased ability to keep track of behaviors that have good or bad outcomes, so you'll be able to pinpoint which ones work well for you
- Increased ability to identify relationships or situations that provoke frequent negative thoughts or feelings

Right now, we'll focus on negative thoughts and feelings, as you'll learn more about handling negative situations in the upcoming weeks. Every time you have a major negative thought or feeling, make an entry in your log as soon as possible. You can use the notebook in which you recorded your quiz scores, an agenda or journal, or even a little notepad that fits easily into a pocket or purse.

We recommend that you keep this log for at least the next month. The number of entries you make will probably depend on how much time you can devote to the program. If possible, about five entries a day would be ideal, but try for at least one a day. Include the following elements in each entry:

Scene. Each log entry begins with a scene. Limit your observations to what you could see and hear. Think of this information as what would hold up in a court. For each detail, ask yourself, "If other people had been there, would they have been able to record this the way I have?" If you can answer yes, write those details *only*—no judgments allowed in this section.

Virginia's Log

Scene: *March 17, in conference room for company meeting. For a number of minutes, I am arguing to the group in favor of one marketing plan. Redford wants another. Redford finally says, "That's enough. This is going on too long! Let's go on!"*

Thoughts: *This is necessary information. Redford is being self-absorbed. He's not listening, really.*

Feelings: *Annoyed, disgusted, disappointed*

Behaviors: *I say, "This is important," and continue what I am saying. I can tell my lips are pursed and jaw clenched.*

Consequences: *Some people squirm. I finish up. Later, someone suggests that Redford and I come back when we've decided this between us.*

Redford's Log

Scene: *I'm putting references into a manuscript I am writing. The stack of journal articles I had referenced is nowhere to be found.*

Thoughts: *Where did I put the damn stuff? Why am I so disorganized? Why was I so lazy?*

Feelings: *Annoyed, frustrated, guilty*

Behaviors: *Go back to Medline to reprint the references.*

Consequences: *It took an extra 2 hours to complete the job. I resolve in the future to put references in as I write the manuscript.*

Thoughts. Your interpretations of the situation have a category all their own, labeled "thoughts." This is where you can record your running internal commentary, based on your observations. This is the place for personal judgments and the shadings that establish your perspective on the situation.

Feelings. When writing this part of your entry, be as specific as you can. If you have trouble, you can start by making an "X" along the positive-negative spectrum if you need to. The more specific you can be when you record your feelings, the greater your abilities will be in determining *exactly* what's upsetting you, which will in turn increase your ability to solve the problem. As a start, we've found that it can be helpful to check the list of universal, possibly universal, and widespread feelings listed in "Everyone Has Emotions" on page 50. You may also want to rate the intensity of your feelings, from very slight — 1 — through exceedingly strong — 10.

Behaviors. Next, record your behaviors: Exactly what did you say or do? Again, it's important to be specific. "I said [the exact words that came out of your mouth]" will be much more helpful to you than writing, "I really told him off!" Also include the way you moved your body or face — "I turned away from him" or "I shut my eyes and shook my head" — as these are important parts of your message.

Your Thoughts and Feelings Log

This log is a handy way to get your thoughts and feelings down on paper and out of your head. Either photocopy this log or duplicate it in your notebook. These entries will become the foundation of your 8-week journey.

Scene: When, where, who, what?
(Describe only the objectively observable facts of the scene in which the thoughts and/or feelings came up.)

_____

_____

Thoughts: What were you thinking?

_____

_____

_____

Feelings: What were you feeling?
(For example, were you angry? Sad? Afraid? Happy? Disgusted? Surprised? Interested? Loving? Ashamed? Or maybe you were aware of only general sensations. Were you anxious? Upset? Pleased? Frustrated? Concerned?)

_____

_____

Behaviors: What did you say or do?

_____

_____

_____

Consequences: What was the outcome of your behavior?

_____

_____

Consequences. The last part of the entry is dedicated to the outcome of the situation, or the consequences. Did your behavior lead to a successful resolution of the situation? Was there no resolution? Or did it make the situation even worse?

Include both the general and the specific. Writing, "The atmosphere was really tense for the next couple of days" is a helpful general observation. "He yelled back, 'You don't know what you're talking about!'" is specific. Both are very useful. As with "thoughts," it's okay to include your interpretation of the outcome here.

When we give a workshop or talk, we always begin the log-keeping exercise by reporting log entries of our own (see "Virginia's Log" and "Redford's Log" on pages 58–59). Seeing our logs, participants may even think, "What gives them the right to be teaching this course? Do they have it all together?" or even "They clearly don't have it all together!" The doubts that others may have about our skills can be especially strong when we facilitate a course or workshop together.

Redford likes to keep his timetables flexible so he can go with the flow and give matters their due. He also may have some pearls of wisdom to share. Virginia likes to get participants talking but stays on schedule, so that all parts of the program get equal emphasis and participants get out on time. She keeps her own comments to a minimum. When Redford goes beyond the previously agreed-upon time allotment for a specific exercise, Virginia gets annoyed. When Virginia requests that he wind up his section, Redford gets annoyed. So the truth is, despite our years of promulgating the skills and trying to practice them ourselves, we do get frustrated with each other—even in front of workshop participants! But if the participants had known us earlier, they'd realize just how much progress we've made.

You can get started by writing at least one log entry right now. For this initial exercise, try to choose an incident that happened within the past few days (or, if it was particularly upsetting and you can recall most of the details, within the past 6 months to a year). Stick to a situation that didn't have as good an outcome as you would have liked. If something about a situation has continued to bother you since it happened, you'll probably get the most out of this lesson by using that example.

As you work through the subsequent weeks, you can use this log entry as a touchstone of learning. As you learn each new skill, ask yourself if it could have been applied to the situation described in the entry and how that might have affected the outcome. As you go forward in the process, try to make a log entry at least once a day. You may find it so helpful that you'd like to do it several times a day. If so, all the better!

If you're not sure where to start, think of a particular relationship (such as with your spouse or a co-worker) or a situation in which you find yourself struggling. Do your entries about this relationship or situation. This will enable you to focus on it as you move through the steps. The entries will also help you explore this area in greater depth. These activities can form the foundation of your work to improve a relationship or situation that you know is a long-term problem for you. Later, you can branch out and include other areas where you'd like to see improvement, but take the first nibble from your most troublesome concern.

MERRISON LEARNS TO STOP STUFFING

After she and her family had been back in Ohio for a year, Merrison decided that at least 50 of those extra 60 pounds had to go.

At first, she defined her problem as those 60 pounds. In retrospect, she could see that the isolation following the births of both children had triggered her weight gains. Moving to Chile had reversed her earlier success, leading her to regain the 10 pounds she had previously lost. She told herself she had been a victim of circumstance.

To achieve her goal, Merrison decided that this time she would enroll in a weight-loss program at a major medical center, and she chose the 1-month resi-

dential program at the Duke Diet and Fitness Center. While she was there, she signed up for a class that taught our program, which is where we met her.

It took awhile for Merrison to get the knack of keeping a log. Focusing on negative situations that provoked negative thoughts and feelings was contrary to her entire nature. How unpleasant! *How negative! Surely only bad people indulged in such putdowns of the world around them and the people in it. And if she joined them in wallowing, she would become—gulp!—a bad person.*

On her first try, Merrison scribbled briefly. Because she had so much difficulty identifying her precise feelings, she began by using the spectrum: She simply observed whether her feelings about the general situations she described were mainly negative, mainly positive, or somewhere in the middle.

From those beginnings, she then learned to be aware of when she was "upset," which was a huge stride for her. Prior to that point, Merrison had really not admitted those kinds of feelings to herself.

Over time, she began to notice that most participants in her workshop responded emotionally when there were crises in their lives. One friend became very angry about how birthday presents to her niece had been handled. Another was clearly very angry with his daughter-in-law, whom he saw as selfish and inflexible because she hadn't gone out to dinner with him and his wife before they left on a long trip out of state. He was annoyed and disgusted.

Merrison began to notice others who reported feeling scared, surprised, happy, or ashamed. All these pleasant people, her friends, experienced negative feelings! She began to give herself permission to have some negative feelings of her own.

Slowly, with dawning awareness, Merrison began to recognize that she felt lonely in her marriage. She began to think that her husband was emotionally withdrawn. When he did speak—which was rare—it was in single, clipped sentences and usually only in response to direct questions. He rarely asked her what she was thinking and never asked what she was feeling. For the past few years, he had rarely looked her squarely in the eyes in a way that said, "It's important to me to be able to get inside you, to know the real you." Didn't he care anymore?

We asked Merrison to focus her attention on one occasion when her husband's behavior really troubled her.

"When I told him about my decision to enroll in the Duke weight-loss program, and he responded, 'That's fine,'" she said.

"And how did you feel when he said that?" we asked.

"I felt really hurt. . . . He didn't seem interested in something so important to me!" In her "feelings" line, she wrote "Hurt." For her "thoughts," she wrote, "He doesn't seem interested in something so important to me!"

Moving on to other areas of her life, Merrison realized that she felt her boss at her part-time job wasn't appreciative enough. We asked, "What's one time recently when your boss failed to appreciate your efforts?"

She had just spent several days on a project that turned out to be difficult. "Just before I came here, my boss piled a lot of extra work on me. I put in extra hours at no additional pay to finish everything," she reported. No thanks expressed by her boss. Merrison went on to report a second incident. On another occasion, she had reorganized some existing folders to make files easier to find—again with no thanks. Instead, her boss asked when she was going to clean up his personal files. He was joking, wasn't he? Surely he was joking!

When we asked how she felt about that, Merrison thought for a second, then said, "Disgusted," looking surprised at her own emphatic reply. Down went that word into her log.

She was on a roll. Her church work was making too many demands on her free time. Choir practice was every Wednesday night. The congregation had at least 200 members, and not all of them were ailing or parenting young children—yet everyone always came to her first to ask for help.

"What's one recent example of your church asking too much?" we asked.

"Right after I finished heading up the fund-raising canvass for this year—which is a lot of work—our minister had the nerve to ask if I would head it up *again next year!" she answered. "How about some appreciation instead of another demand?"*

"Did you have any reaction when he said that?"

"I guess I was annoyed . . . no . . . actually, I was really pissed!" She looked around at her fellow classmates, who nodded and smiled. Buoyed by her own energy, she wrote down "annoyed." (Maybe "pissed" would have been a bit too strong for gentle Merrison!)

At this point, Merrison moved on to the "behaviors" entry for each situation. She was surprised to note that after each of these specific incidents, she had eaten more than usual. By keeping her log, she was beginning to see exactly how her extra pounds were linked to "stuffing" her own negative feelings. It was the beginning of a breakthrough.

Back home, Merrison practiced her new coping skills in situations at work. She realized that at least twice a day, her boss annoyed her by being demanding yet unappreciative. Using her new evaluation tools, she concluded she didn't want that. She searched around and luckily found a new job that she enjoyed much more.

Six months after her time at the Diet and Fitness Center, people at church were still coming to Merrison first. She decided to take charge there, too. Applying other skills about saying no (you'll learn these skills in Week 5), Merrison established a policy of not responding until she was fully aware of what she thought and felt. Sometimes, she found that she knew right away; on other occasions, she needed a day or two to weigh her thoughts and feelings and ask herself some evaluative questions. Sometimes she eventually answered yes, other times she said no. The net effect was that she started taking on only those projects that really interested her and in which she took pleasure. For the rest, they'd have to find someone else.

As a result of her stay at the center and her continuing emotional work, Merrison eventually did lose 50 pounds. She and her dietitian tailored an eating plan that helped her develop a taste for foods that were filling but low in calories. Instead of her former standbys of pasta with cream sauces, desserts, butter, and fried foods, she learned to choose fruits and vegetables, lean cuts of meat, whole grains, and salads with low-calorie dressings. She drank lots of water. Every morning at the center, she swam laps in the pool, and every evening, she walked for a couple of miles.

At home, Merrison established similar eating patterns, continued the evening walks, and kept writing in her log. A year later, 40 of those pounds still were off. She and her husband were spending more time together, and there seemed to be fewer "silent treatments" on both sides. Merrison had taken the initiative in rekindling their emotional connection by taking a chance: She decided that each day, she would tell her husband a few things that had happened to her, including her positive and negative reactions to each event. Once she saw that he was open to hearing her thoughts and feelings on other matters, Merrison got up the courage to start letting her husband know when she felt lonely or overworked or just plain unappreciated. She was delighted to see that rather than getting upset, he was opening up a little bit, reporting some of his day's activities and even a few of his positive and negative reactions to what was happening at home. Gradually, Merrison's sweet tooth was sated by happy memories, and her soul began to fill up with moments of true connection.

Week 1 Recap

1. Realize that everyone has feelings, whether they're aware of them or not.

2. Use awareness of feelings to savor the moment or as a signal to pay attention right then to what is happening around you.

3. To learn this skill, begin to keep a log of thoughts and feelings in situations that evoke them. Record:

Scene: What were the objectively observable facts?

Thoughts: What did you say to yourself?

Feelings: Were you feeling angry? Sad? Fearful? Full of joy? Disgusted? Some other emotion? (Perhaps you will need to begin with a more general sensation, such as "upset," or even just "mainly positive" or "mainly negative.")

Behaviors: What did you say or do? (If you did nothing, record that as well.)

Consequences: What was the outcome of your behavior?

CHAPTER 4

WEEK 2: WEIGH THE EVIDENCE

This week, you'll learn to use our system for thinking before you act. When you experience negative thoughts or feelings, you'll learn to stop, carefully weigh the evidence—both objective and subjective—and decide on the best course of action. It's this pause that will empower you to consider which options would result in the wisest path. Sometimes your response will require action, and sometimes it won't. But the pause and self-questioning process guarantee that on average, you will respond in the manner that's most likely to achieve your goals, given all of the options available.

The adage "Physician, heal thyself" played a big part in the development of our program. When Redford was doing his research on hostility and health several decades ago, he began to see that he had many of the key health-damaging characteristics—a cynical mistrust of others, sudden bursts of anger, and an occasionally abrasive interpersonal style—mentioned in the first chapter. This realization, combined with Virginia's pressure on him to change, led him to modify his behavior in ways that were crucial for his health.

We find it's always helpful to include our own stories when we teach workshops—as we've mentioned, we know the system works, because it saved our marriage! Here is Redford's story, in his own words.

I guess you could say that I embody extremes. After high school, I rarely exercised until I was in my late fifties, but now I work out six times a week, both for my health and to maintain the muscle I inherited from my sturdy Welsh forebears. I love to have fun—I watch movies and read, and I'm a fanatical fan of the Duke basketball team—yet I check my e-mail several times a day and work on papers into the night. Many people have told me that I react with "gusto" to the world around me. I have to admit, they're right: Sometimes it's with enthusiasm, other times with anger, but always with gusto!

As I grew up, I had my strengths and my challenge areas. I was blessed with a solid feeling of confidence, which may have grown out of being so dearly loved as a child. I also spent every summer with adoring grandparents and two not-yet-married aunts in an idyllic small town in eastern North Carolina. Their house faced the courthouse square. Neighbors were close friends; everyone knew everyone else's business, for better and worse.

The rest of the year, I lived in a migrant labor camp, where my father was the manager. The little town nearby was full of rows of white clapboard and brick houses, each with pretty flowers in the yard. My home was not as picture-perfect; I slept in a small alcove right next to the front door of our one-bedroom house. The once dark green paint on the outside had become faded, as had the paint on the camp store.

As a child, I watched a lot of the fallout from my father's drinking problems and my mother's inability to come to terms with his behavior when he was drinking. Let me be clear about one thing at the outset: No matter how bad things got, their love for me was never in doubt. Much of the time, however, their problems meant I was left on my own. I could always persuade my father to take me to the movies on both Saturday and Sunday (when things tended to be worse at home). He would drop me off in front of the theater with money for a ticket and a cab ride home. Sometimes there weren't many cabs, and I had to wait a long time before one came by. To keep from feeling overwhelmed by my loneliness and fears, I would often daydream about things—the home run I was going to hit with the bases loaded at the next softball game, or the A I was going to get on the next test.

Or I'd think about Christmas, when I'd get to go back to my grandparents' and that small North Carolina town. Those were always happy times—including no drinking problems for me to worry about.

Slowly and surely, I was learning lessons: Other people can't be trusted to take care of you, but if you work hard yourself and shut out the rest of the world, you can take charge of your own fate. The latter lesson probably helped me get a scholarship to college, but I was also learning not to focus on how I was treating others. By shutting them out so their actions had a minimal effect on me, I was also failing to observe and process the effects my own actions were having on others.

Of course, my biology also went into the mix. As a natural-born hot reactor, I always felt full of energy. On the good side, I was usually immediately aware of my thoughts and feelings. New ideas excited me, so I was naturally very happy to compliment those whose work and thoughts I respected. Yet my way of coping with my home situation meant that I was also constantly on the lookout for the mistakes of others, and I often found them. As a hot reactor, I got riled and lashed out.

Redford Needed to Quiet His Eruptions

I had done what I needed to do to get myself educated and beyond my early home situation. This had been my priority, and I'd succeeded. But a new and different set of challenges lay ahead when, right after college, I married Virginia.

Virginia wanted a close, intimate relationship in which she and I would depend on each other. Early in our marriage, I sometimes found myself exploding at the slightest provocation. One evening, I stomped out of the dining area of our little living room and into the kitchen, dinner plate in hand. The rice casserole with nuts and mushrooms wasn't hot through and through! I plopped my portion back into the pan and thrust the pan back into the oven, slamming the door. Another night, I told Virginia the chili was "ruined" by the extra can of tomatoes that diluted the other ingredients. Or the laundry was still damp. Or the newspaper hadn't been folded properly. Or Virginia drove too slowly. There were lots of occasions for outbursts.

Only after I'd reacted would I realize that Virginia's feelings were hurt. Then I'd be sorry, but Virginia, who was still hurt and not yet good at sticking up for herself, would sulk. (We'll see how our program helped Virginia conquer her problems with sulking in Week 5.) Both of us began to see my outbursts as a problem.

Likewise, I was encountering moments during my medical training that indicated I needed to change. I had no problem controlling my anger around patients or senior staff, but I was less successful with fellow trainees or other health care providers, such as nurses. During the first two years of medical school, I'd been rewarded when I spoke up to challenge my teachers, often with "probing" questions that some might interpret as pushy. When I began my internal medicine clerkship on the hospital wards in my third year, the expectations were different, as were the responses to my outspoken behavior. I nearly flunked this first clerkship at the hospital because as a medical student, I was too ready to criticize the interns and residents (see "Redford's Log" on page 72).

These outbursts were harming my career. Behaving this way was at odds with the kind of physician I wanted to be, and I began to realize that without better temper control, I might not get into a good internship, residency, or fellowship program.

Other professional interests also pointed me toward change. By the time I was in training, the best medical practice was not only focusing on curing disease or disability, it was starting to emphasize prevention as well. The medical profession was beginning to extend this proactive focus to include emotional fitness, and I realized that I needed to practice what I was beginning to preach.

Even years after I came to realize all this, I still had trouble controlling my impulses. Outbursts still happened over trivial matters. Our daughter Jennifer dropped the contents of her ice-cream cone. Someone in my office turned up the thermostat on the air conditioner. I'd left the article I was reading in a medical journal at the office. The episodes kept occurring, but I was learning. I was making progress. Still, my outbursts were frequent enough to make me realize I wasn't in control.

> *Redford's Log*
>
> **Scene:** *Morning rounds with senior attending physician, the ward resident, two interns, and three other medical students. The attending asks one of the interns whether the patient should be treated with drug X.*
>
> **Thoughts:** *Drug X! That's the last thing you want to give a patient who has this condition; it would probably kill her within 2 days. The attending is trying to trick the intern on this one.*
>
> **Feelings:** *Excited, exhilarated*
>
> **Behaviors:** *While the intern is still pondering the question, I interject, "Give her drug X and she'll be dead by day after tomorrow!"*
>
> **Consequences:** *The intern looks embarrassed, then says, "I knew that, that was just what I was going to say!" The resident scowls at me. That night, the resident doesn't call me in when a really interesting patient is admitted.*
>
> *When I get my grade at the end of the clerkship, I'm surprised to learn that I barely passed. I have to do an extra rotation—taking care the whole time to be super-hardworking and display the humility appropriate to my status—to repair the damage from my outspoken, pushy behavior.*

All around me were indications that this behavior had health implications. My own research at about this time showed that a group of doctors who had answered a personality test in medical school in ways that indicated they were suspicious of the motives of others, who frequently became angry when they detected others' bad behavior, and who didn't hesitate to let them hear about it were seven times more likely to die by age 50 than their more easygoing counterparts.[1] I realized that I was behaving just like the hostile doctors in my research!

These research findings, and Virginia's rising dissatisfaction with the way I was treating her and our children, made me realize that for the sake of my relationships and my health, I needed to learn to evaluate situations before taking any other action. I needed to develop an organized means of helping myself to decide between trying to get over my negative thoughts and feelings and trying to change situations that were causing me distress. The process we developed would form the heart of our program.

BRING IN THE JURY

Thoughts and feelings, when left to fester inside, are really only dangerous to ourselves, which is certainly reason enough to deal with them. Thoughtless behaviors can cause even more damage. We may act against our self-interest before thinking the matter through. If others are affected, our relationships may begin to suffer.

Stuffers, like Merrison in Week 1, need to learn to recognize their feelings, primarily to protect themselves and their own needs, but also to enrich and strengthen their honest relationships with others. Once they accomplish this, they will still need to evaluate their behavioral options. The end result will be:

- Fewer festering feelings
- More problems solved
- Better treatment from others
- Self-protection against being taken advantage of

Hot reactors, or "volcanoes," like Redford, are very much in touch with their feelings—in fact, they have that part sewn up! They need to practice evaluating before acting. Otherwise, volcanoes may have to deal with the fallout from their own eruptions, including:

- Too-frequent fight-or-flight responses, which can damage the body in all the ways discussed in the first chapter
- Loved ones who feel hurt by outbursts and over time may distance themselves from the volcano

- Friends and colleagues who may avoid contact; after all, who needs the stress of being around a volcano?

- Employees or staff who are likely to feel cautious and distant, rather than motivated to go the extra mile

- Real crises that go unnoticed and unresolved because the volcano is dismissed as acting the same as usual

Volcanoes portion out energy unwisely. It makes little difference whether the matter is important, their position is justifiable, or change is possible. Nor do they consider the big picture. As a result, they spend a lot of time ineffectively spinning their wheels. They need to think before they react. Otherwise, misplaced anger and other unconstructive reactions are sure to destroy their relationships. We've developed the following system as a handy way of working through your feelings in a constructive manner that's likely to bring about the best, most positive reaction.

KNOW THE I AM WORTH IT QUESTIONS

Having a set of specific guidelines to follow when you have to decide how to react to a stressful situation would be useful to everyone, not just for people prone to outbursts. Why? The guidelines give you a systematic way of evaluating the situation that takes away most of the guesswork.

We call our four evaluating questions the I AM WORTH IT system (you'll see why shortly). By the time you get to the fourth question, you will have figured out your wisest response to the current situation.

The I AM WORTH IT questions are:

1. Is the matter Important to me? You are the expert here. Working with the data you've amassed in your Thoughts and Feelings Log, take a good look at the whole picture. Obviously, on some level, the matter is important to you, or you wouldn't even bother committing it to paper. But when you see it written down, you may find yourself thinking, "That's not such a big deal" or "Boy, am I getting excited for nothing." On the other hand, maybe you realize, "This is important to me."

If you decide that no, this matter isn't important, stop! You need to move on to deflection skills you'll learn in Week 3.

If you decide that yes, it is important to you, go to the second question.

2. Is what I'm feeling and/or thinking Appropriate to the facts of the situation? When you ask this question, stick to what you can see or hear, not your interpretation of what has happened. If you're unsure of your answer, think about how you would respond if a friend or relative presented you with the same facts and then asked if her reaction was appropriate. Or you can ask someone you respect if he would have reacted as you did when confronted with a similar situation.

If you decide that your feelings aren't appropriate to the situation, stop! You need to move on and use deflection skills.

If you decide that your thoughts and feelings are appropriate, continue to the third question.

3. Is this situation Modifiable in a positive way? Based on everything you know about the event in question, should you be able to change the situation? For example, being caught in a traffic jam on a rainy day is not usually something you can fix. On the other hand, if your partner has told you she thinks one of your ideas is stupid, perhaps she could be persuaded to stop making remarks like that. (In a case like this, your log entry situation may not be modifiable this time, as the other person has already said or done whatever caused your negative feeling. You may be able to conclude, though, that the next time a similar situation arises, you could devise a way to persuade the other person to behave differently.)

If you decide the situation is not modifiable in a positive way, stop! Shift your attention to deflection skills.

If you determine that yes, the situation is modifiable, move on to the fourth and final question.

4. When I balance the needs of others and myself, is taking action WORTH IT? Ah, this is sometimes the rub. You may have three yeses, then get to the last question and realize that you need to weigh the likely consequences from all perspectives. Perhaps taking action has too much of a downside. However, just as often, you may come to understand how much you really want to do something about the situation.

Consider your relationship with the other person or people, their feelings, and your own feelings and needs. Weigh the pros and cons. When you look at all aspects of the situation, is taking action really worth it?

For example, let's say your teenage daughter asks you to take her to the mall. You're busy at the moment, and you have plans of your own, so you explain why you won't be able to take her. She screams, "You don't care about me at all!"

Your heart starts to pound (how dare she speak to you like that!), but when you ask yourself the four questions, you decide that in the scheme of things, in a teenager's fickle, changing world, while it may be Important, your response Appropriate, and the situation somewhat Modifiable (you could demand an apology or even ground her), this matter is not **WORTH IT.** You know you have to pick your battles, and you've limited yourself to one confrontation per weekend—this weekend, it's going to be about her room.

Driving down the highway, you come upon a construction zone. Drivers are instructed to pull into the right lane, but one car stays in the left lane, speeding by until just before the cutoff point. He's slightly ahead of you, and he tries to pull in front of you. The matter is important to you—the jerk! Your feelings of anger are appropriate. If you speed up, you may be able to keep him from cutting in, so the situation is possibly modifiable. But if you try that and he continues, you'll crash into the side of his car. You conclude it's not worth it to take that chance!

In this case, the **WORTH IT** question saves you from taking action that may not turn out well. Think of some other situations—at work, for example—when you might get three yeses, but it still won't be worth it to take action.

If, after thoroughly weighing this question, you're leaning toward yes, you can employ the strategies we discuss in Weeks 4 and 5.

To see the entire four-question system at once, take a look at the flow chart on page 78. Twenty years of experience with this process has shown us time and again that the moment taken to ask yourself the I AM WORTH IT questions practically guarantees that your actions will be effective and in line with your long-term beliefs, needs, and goals. Let's look at some examples to see the I AM WORTH IT questions in action.

Selma is having a bad day at the insurance company where she works. All morning, she's been busy, asking questions and typing intake information as people file claims. Just before Selma's break, her co-worker Julia's computer shuts down. This means a delay before Selma's break. She's furious at both Julia and the situation, so she makes the following log entry.

Scene: Thursday, February 10, 10:15, at work station. Julia tells me that her computer has shut down.
Thoughts: She froze that screen on purpose. Why won't our supervisor let us switch computers—she's a witch, too. I hate this place. I need a break.
Feelings: Anger, disgust. On a scale of 1 to 10, about a 9 on anger and a 10 on disgust.

Because Selma is in Week 2 of this program, she doesn't say anything to Julia yet (so as of now, there are no behaviors or consequences to record). Instead, she takes a deep breath and says to herself, "I AM WORTH IT!" This reminds her to ask the four questions.

1. Is this Important? "Yes. I need that break."

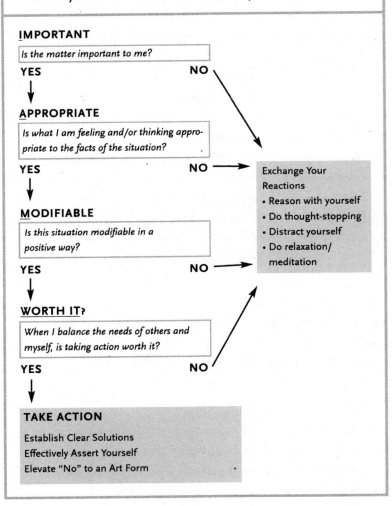

The I AM WORTH IT *Questions*

When you ask the I AM WORTH IT questions, consider the objective facts of the situation and your reaction to it.

IMPORTANT

Is the matter important to me?

YES   NO

APPROPRIATE

Is what I am feeling and/or thinking appropriate to the facts of the situation?

YES   NO ⟶

MODIFIABLE

Is this situation modifiable in a positive way?

YES   NO ⟶

WORTH IT?

When I balance the needs of others and myself, is taking action worth it?

YES   NO

Exchange Your Reactions
- Reason with yourself
- Do thought-stopping
- Distract yourself
- Do relaxation/ meditation

TAKE ACTION

Establish Clear Solutions
Effectively Assert Yourself
Elevate "No" to an Art Form

2. Is this Appropriate? Selma finds it helpful to repeat the heart of her log entry within the question itself: "Is it appropriate for me to be annoyed and disgusted at Julia because her computer locked up?"

She thinks about it and realizes she has a no: "Well, it's not really appropriate. Julia can't help it that her computer screen froze. Mine did that the other day." But this also helps Selma realize that she may be angry at someone else: her supervisor, who has a rule that co-workers can't share computers. So Selma asks the question again, a little differently this time: "Is it appropriate for me to be annoyed and disgusted at Marcia for making a rule that none of us who gather intake information can borrow each other's computers?"

She realizes that answer is also no. "I wouldn't want anybody borrowing my computer. Suppose somebody messed up," she thinks. "So I guess I understand why Marcia can't let us share computers."

Selma begins again, building on that conclusion: "Is it appropriate for me to be annoyed and disgusted that computers can break down?"

Now she has a yes, so Selma goes on to her third question—but centering *only* around the feeling of being angry and disgusted that computers can break down.

3. Is this Modifiable? "Is there anything I can do that will change the fact that computers can lock up?"

Here Selma gets a no. She realizes, "Not even computer experts have been able to pull that one off yet!"

Selma has concluded that her anger and disgust at Julia and Marcia aren't really appropriate, and there's nothing she can do to modify the fact that computer glitches do happen, so she stops there and doesn't ask the fourth question. In the end, because she can't change the situation, she decides to try to get over her initial negative feelings. It would be smarter to put energy into calming herself down.

Fred's situation is different. Just as he's about to leave work, his friend Wayne asks him for a $20 loan for something he needs to buy on the way home. Fred has loaned Wayne money before, but he has a sinking feeling this time. He can't put his finger on exactly why, but he knows he doesn't feel good about it. So Fred mentally does a log entry.

Scene: Wayne has asked me to lend him $20. (Fred then remembers that Wayne still owes him $10 from a few weeks ago.)
Thoughts: He still hasn't paid me back from the last time.
Feelings: Bad. (As Fred practices recognizing his emotions, he'll begin to identify what he's feeling with greater precision. This is a good start.)

Those are negative thoughts and feelings, all right! So Fred asks Wayne to give him a couple of minutes to think about it. He takes a deep breath and silently says to himself, "I AM WORTH IT" to remind himself to move on to the questions.

1. Is it Important? "Yes! It's my money!"

2. Is it Appropriate? "Yes. I would expect to pay somebody back before making another request. Wayne will just have to get into the habit of going by the bank."

3. Is it Modifiable? "Yes, it is. I can say no."

4. Is it **WORTH IT**? "Friendship is important, but it's a two-way street. Maybe Wayne should do something for me next—so yes!"

When Fred considers both Wayne's needs and his own, he realizes that taking some action would serve several purposes. First, he wouldn't feel as bad (and he'd be able to hold on to more of his money). Second, he realizes that in situations like this, Wayne needs to learn to rely on himself, not on his friends. So Fred says he won't be able to lend him the money.

Two situations, the same set of I AM WORTH IT questions, and different answers. Selma and Fred each used the questions to get a quick read on the appropriateness of their first instincts. In assessing the state of affairs before figuring out what to do, Selma avoided a display of temper that would lower her esteem in the eyes of her co-workers, her supervisor, and herself. What's more, she avoided putting a strain on her body. Fred protected himself from being taken advantage of. And who knows, he may even get his first loan back!

USE THE I AM WORTH IT QUESTIONS BEFORE ACTING

From now on, whenever you're confronted with a situation that provokes negative thoughts or feelings, ask yourself the I AM WORTH IT questions *before* doing anything else. This will set your compass toward your best course. Those few extra moments of pause are invaluable because they'll save you time—and relationships!—in the long run.

Now it's time for you to try. Copy the blank template from "Your I AM WORTH IT Worksheet" on page 82 into your notebook. Begin by practicing on two of the Thoughts and Feelings Log entries you wrote up last week.

Remember, the examples you've chosen are in retrospect. As such, while they can be illustrative, instructive, and perhaps a bit interesting, they can't have a major impact on your life as you live it right now. To do that, you need to apply the I AM WORTH IT questions the next time you experience negative thoughts and feelings—*before* you take any other action.

As you work through the program, you'll see how integral these four questions are and how critical it is to make a habit of asking them. Use them as a touchstone in sticky situations. Promise yourself that before you do anything—whether blowing up, like Redford, or chowing down, like Merrison—you will take a few seconds to be aware of the objective facts, your thoughts, and your feelings and then run through the questions. If it works for you, treat it like a mantra or a prayer—anything that will remind you to pause, take a moment for your own thoughts and feelings, and work through them internally before acting on them.

(continued on page 84)

Your I AM WORTH IT *Worksheet*

Use this worksheet to help you answer the questions and determine your next steps in any situation in which you have negative thoughts or feelings. Copy this template into your notebook.

Next, look at your Thoughts and Feelings Log and ask the I AM WORTH IT questions for each entry. Would your actions have been different if you had asked these questions first?

Scene:

_____

_____

_____

_____

_____

_____

_____

_____

_____

Thoughts:

_____

_____

_____

_____

_____

_____

Feelings:

_____
_____
_____
_____

Important?

_____
_____
_____
_____

Appropriate?

_____
_____
_____
_____

Modifiable?

_____
_____
_____
_____

WORTH IT?

_____
_____
_____
_____

If you try to ask the I AM WORTH IT questions several times a day, you'll no doubt learn to ask them more routinely, and the whole process will feel less awkward. Reaching the goal of continuous application will take attention and work; such behavior isn't automatic for most of us. Behaving this way may not feel easy at all, but soon it will become second nature — and that's when you'll begin to reap the benefits of a life lived in control.

REDFORD LEARNS TO TAMP DOWN THE VOLCANO

Many of the clinical studies in the field of stress-related medicine — both Redford's and those of other researchers — have found that a cynical mistrust of others, angry feelings, and aggressive outbursts increase the risk of cardiovascular disease. We know that depression can also lead to increased risk.

While he was spending so much of his time over the past few decades conducting this research, Redford was also putting considerable energy into thinking before acting on his first impulses. Let's hear the rest of his story.

I've found that the easiest situations to address have been those that had the potential to develop into crises. For example, I was able to control myself and not throw a fit when the Medical Center Institutional Review Board — the governing body that must grant ethical approval before research can be done — misplaced my application for several months. (When I asked myself the I AM WORTH IT questions, I realized I couldn't change what had happened, and even if I could, it wouldn't have been worth it.)

Then there was the time that, despite feeling ready to go through the roof, I managed to quickly get over my initial reaction when our son Lloyd's Doberman puppy urinated on our expensive rug. (The four questions told me that my feelings were indeed important and appropriate at the time, but the situation was not modifiable in that instance — the dog couldn't really take back its action!) I did ask Lloyd to monitor his puppy more closely in the future, but I didn't blow up.

The real test was a daylong delay out of the Raleigh-Durham airport during an ice storm. Now, weather delays are a fact of nature—this much I know. But when the delays were announced in fits and starts that stretched from 10 A.M. to 9 P.M. . . . .well, let's just say I can think of a million better ways to spend my time. The four questions helped me stay rational and move beyond my irritation. ("I must be in New York tomorrow; no other flights out on other airlines; equally problematic to leave the airport to catch a train or drive. Important, Appropriate. Only Modifiable by train or car—and that's not WORTH IT!") I ended up taking the earliest flight the next morning, and all was well.

Once I tackled these crisis situations, I started moving into areas in which my reactions to minor annoyances were having effects on my relationships. I consistently try to employ the I AM WORTH IT questions hour by hour, day by day in minor as well as major matters. My goal is that in most situations evoking negative feelings, I can think first before acting—and I can honestly say I've been achieving my goal. The newspaper is wrinkled (not important). The soup isn't hot enough (modifiable by a quick trip to the microwave and worth it to do that). The car in front of me is moving too slowly for my preference (not worth sending Virginia into a tizzy by passing when a car in the other lane is approaching too close for her comfort). Supper isn't ready (not important). Virginia's not ready to go to church yet, but there's still plenty of time before we need to leave (not appropriate). The wooden deck is beginning to rot, despite resealing (not modifiable).

I'm especially gratified (and relieved!) when friends and professional colleagues tell me I'm much more "mellow" than I was before. That's a real achievement for me! Even Virginia claims I'm much more pleasant to live with. Do I always ask the four questions when I'm upset? No, especially not when I'm tired, stressed, or jet-lagged. But I can tell, from both my relationships and my health, that I'm making a lot of progress. Here are some of my pet projects—areas where I'm trying to ask the I AM WORTH IT questions before acting on impulse.

- Correcting someone else's pronunciation (not important, not worth it)
- Interrupting (not worth it)

Field Guide

THE GROCERY STORE

You have only 20 minutes to get in and out of the grocery store. You'd planned to grab a pizza for dinner with your partner. Since your son will be home from college for the weekend, you plan on making a few of his favorite snacks. And you have to pick up some ingredients for dinner tomorrow night.

Your list is short, and you move through the aisles quickly. You congratulate yourself on your efficiency.

Then you're ready to check out. You normally opt for the automatic checkout because you can just whisk your items across the sensor and bag them yourself. Nothing to it. You can do this in less than 2 minutes—except that one of the four checkout stations seems to be broken, and two of the others are currently occupied by people who appear to be unfamiliar with using them. Plus, eight people are in line in front of you.

You clearly have more than 10 items, so you can't go through the express line. You survey the regular lines. Aisle 4 looks best, so you wheel your cart over there.

Of course, once you've committed, every other line moves faster, but it's too late to take back your decision. You're annoyed and disgusted at how inefficient the store management is—they have no consideration for the customers!

Now, wait a minute! This situation is getting you agitated. It's time for the I AM WORTH IT questions.

1. Is it **I**mportant to me whether I get out of the store now or 10 minutes from now? You answer yes.

2. Is it **A**ppropriate for me to be annoyed and disgusted? Considering this is the second time it's happened this week, you answer yes.

3. Can I **M**odify this situation? You consider this and answer, "Well, I could dump eight items or ask someone to let me break into a line."

4. When I balance the needs of everyone—myself, my partner, my son, the other shoppers, the grocer who will have to put whatever I dump back on the shelves—is taking action **WORTH IT**? "Dumping items is out—I want every item in my cart. And I hate it when people break ahead of others in line," you think. "The other shoppers are in a hurry, too. And I'll bet my family would rather have a serene me than extra snacks anyway. I'll either get to preparing those snacks, or I won't—it's not that big a deal!"

As you continue to reason with yourself, you realize that you were acting as if this were a matter of prime importance, and now that you've gone through the four questions, you see that it's not even close.

- Beginning to eat before others are ready (not appropriate)
- Blowing the horn when the person ahead of me doesn't respond to a green light quickly enough (not important)

Your biology and life experiences may make asking the I AM WORTH IT questions hard work, but the rewards of meeting this challenge are immense. If you stick to asking these questions, you'll almost assuredly be rewarded eventually by wasting less energy in fighting annoyances that are only trivial. You'll have a built-in censor that prevents you from behaving ridiculously. You won't spin your wheels pointlessly. And you're likely to have better relations with others. Not a bad payoff!

Week 2 Recap

1. Whenever you're aware of experiencing a negative thought and/or feeling, stop and write or mentally construct a Thoughts and Feelings Log to help you observe the objective facts of the situation (Skill 1).

2. Next, ask four questions:
   - Is this matter Important to me?
   - Is what I am feeling and/or thinking Appropriate to the facts of the situation?
   - Is this situation Modifiable in a positive way?
   - When I balance the needs of others and myself, is taking action WORTH IT?

3. If you get four yeses, resolve to take action (skills you will learn in Weeks 4 and 5); if you get any no answers, resolve to change your reaction (Skill 3, featured next week).

WEEK 3: GAIN CONTROL OF YOUR REACTIONS

This week, you'll learn how to prevent emotional spillover into the aftermath of upsetting situations. There's no gain in remaining in a wired state of hypervigilance when a stressful situation is over, so you'll learn to change your body state. It's counterproductive to wallow in negativity when you've answered no to any of the I AM WORTH IT questions, so you'll learn to take action to reduce the negative thoughts and feelings you're experiencing. As a result, both your body and your relationships are likely to become healthier.

By the time Jerry Flanagan had worked for almost two decades on a large city police force, his hair had thinned, his freckles had faded, and he had acquired a bit of a paunch. He owed some of that expanded girth to fast food bolted down between calls when he was on duty. On occasion, after an especially stressful shift, he would eat a whole pint of ice cream to help him calm down. The beers he shared with his buddies after some shifts also added calories.

A lieutenant in a middle-management position, Jerry supervised other officers, spending part of his time at the station and part on patrol. He felt pressure from the captains and commanders who were his superiors and issued directives that he carried out, whether he approved of their dictums or not. As for the men and women he oversaw, he found that supervising some officers was easy, but others were a challenge. Correct that: Some were a pain in the butt!

On patrol, Jerry covered plenty of action in unsafe neighborhoods. Danger could lurk anywhere. He remained hyperalert all the time he was on duty, using his peripheral vision to help him spot illegal activity or possible threats. He knew all too well that the gang member you don't see when you're frisking his friend is the one who could gun you down.

On too many nights, one or more serious situations arose that had to be dealt with. Young kids carrying guns and smoking dope. Gang shootings. Armed robberies. Domestic violence. Prostitutes soliciting tricks and buying drugs. Mentally ill citizens who would have been institutionalized 40 years ago but now wander the streets. (One guy thought that he had married Britney Spears and that Elvis had attended the wedding. How long would it be until he walked in front of a speeding car—maybe even a police car involved in a high-speed chase?)

Three plaques hung on the wall at the district station, honoring former colleagues who were killed in the line of duty. Jerry had known them all. The plaques were a reminder of the split-second decisions he and the officers he supervised had to make in potentially life-threatening situations: Do I need to fire my gun? If I do, there will be media and the courts to contend with. Suppose a bullet ricochets and hits a bystander? If I don't shoot, will I put myself and another officer in danger?

Despite the exceptionally high stress inherent in being a police lieutenant, Jerry felt good about his work. "This is not just a job," he'd say. "This is who I am." He believed that everyone deserves to feel safe, and he did what he could to make that a reality. He was proud of that.

But the stress had gotten to Jerry, straining his most intimate relationships and compromising his health. He didn't feel close to his children, and he often argued with his wife. He was completely out of breath every time he climbed a couple of flights of stairs. Occasionally, when he was in a very stressful situation or after climbing those steps, he thought fleetingly that he felt a slight pain in his chest.

Jerry Needed to Stop Overreacting

Jerry felt he had a mission to serve and protect. He wanted to do a good job; that much was clear. But in his efforts to stay vigilant, he remained permanently charged, and he was allowing the stresses innate to his job to affect his whole life.

Jerry's home life had degenerated over the past decade. His 14-year-old son, Mitch, edged as close to the line of mouthing off as he could get away with. Jerry cringed each time he saw the short skirts and tight T-shirts his 12-year-old daughter, Kate, favored—they were way too similar to what the prostitutes wore. Sure, he could make Kate wear something else, but that would lead to an argument with his wife, who thought the way their daughter dressed was okay. Both of these situations upset Jerry a great deal.

When he and Dora were first married, they'd been happy. She had been proud that he was a police officer. But once the kids were in school and the expenses started piling up, she had taken a job. Since then, she'd seemed pretty grouchy about it. Sure, they needed the money, but Jerry thought she no longer seemed to appreciate how stressful police work was.

The couple argued about plenty of things: who would discipline the kids, do the grocery shopping, clean up the house, cook dinner, and finish folding the laundry. Dora said she was working harder than Jerry, and he needed to pick up a fair share of the load. Little things were really getting to him, such as the dripping faucets, the spots on the laundry from magic markers left in shirt pockets, and the dirty dishes in the sink.

Almost every day, Dora would rant that Jerry didn't seem very interested in her and the kids. He protested, but he had to admit that he was often preoccupied, reliving a shootout or a drug raid. The truth was he had a better time when he stopped by the bar after a shift. ("Choir practice," everyone called it.) Besides, after a long day, he was physically and emotionally drained. At the station, Jerry was always on edge and ready for action, so he occasionally blew up at someone—the dispatcher, the desk sergeant, or anyone else who happened by.

Not only were Jerry's relationships at work and at home suffering, so was his health. Now, for most people, just the thought of being involved in a gunfight is enough to reduce them to jelly. In contrast, Jerry was trained to react quickly and professionally, according to established protocol. Because he was well aware of how much danger he was in, each time Jerry responded, his heart beat faster, his blood pressure shot up, and stress hormones, such as adrenaline, were released into his bloodstream. His body also stopped processing sugar. These changes intensified as the danger increased, but they were always present.

In crisis situations, these reactions served a very important, protective purpose: They intensified his vigilance and diminished his reaction time. Unfortunately for Jerry's health and relationships, however, the residue from the adrenaline rushes remained after his shift was over. In many situations when Jerry was off-duty, he either overreacted or didn't react at all. Dora complained that he often didn't seem "there," yet sometimes he would become angry at the littlest slight. In either state, Jerry's body was suffering from the toxic aftermath of the hypervigilance essential to his work.

People who apply to be police officers have to pass mental and physical tests as well as background checks to qualify. In numbers greater than suggested by their initial strong profiles, some police officers become so overwhelmed by their demanding, stressful jobs that they turn to alcohol or promiscuity to cope. Rates for divorce and even suicide are also higher. Jerry didn't see himself in danger of any of that, but the stress was causing a downward slide in his life outside of work.

GET OVER IT

We're going to take a big leap here and assume that your job doesn't include wrestling bad guys or engaging in gun battles every day. But biochemically, stress is stress, whether you're staying vigilant to try to stop a robbery or keep your 3-year-old from running out into traffic.

You need to know how to turn off that hypervigilance as well as those negative thoughts and feelings. Remaining in heightened states of anxiety or stress sets you up for serious long-term relationship and health problems.

Any time you answer no to one of the I AM WORTH IT questions, you've begun the process of reasoning with yourself. On your own—without anyone forcing you to answer in these ways—you've admitted to yourself that:

1. The situation that provoked your negative thoughts and/or feelings is not Important, or

2. Your reaction is not Appropriate, or

3. You can't Modify the situation, or

4. It wouldn't be **WORTH IT** to try.

Congratulations! Simply by deciding to clarify your own thinking about a given situation, you've mastered the first step in gaining control. In making this questioning a habit, you will ultimately get more out of life because you'll cut to the heart of what's truly bugging you, as well as not waste time and energy on situations that may not have positive outcomes.

Having reached this admirable, forward-thinking conclusion, you now have to get over it. Several strategies that we worked on with Jerry can help you, too.

First, Try Reasoning with Yourself

We've found that one of the best first methods to help you get over your initial negative feelings is to follow up the I AM WORTH IT questions with self-talk. Indeed, research has shown that people can change their feelings and thoughts by using this kind of tactic. Although it's most often used to combat depression, the technique can be useful in addressing other negative states as well, such as hostility and disgust.[1] Here are some examples that can work for each of your no answers in a variety of circumstances.

- "I've concluded that the matter is *not important.* I need to think about what will happen inside my body if I stay upset. I don't want to measure out my life in moments of anger over something I've decided is insignificant."

- "I can see now that my initial reaction was hasty and *not appropriate.* I reacted before I'd thought the matter through. My mind has now done its work, and I need to trust that and listen to what I've figured out. I need to chill out."

- "No matter what I do, I *can't modify* this situation. Therefore, I need to let it go. Any other course would be counterproductive and just plain senseless!"

- "I've weighed the pros and cons here. Taking action could have a large downside. It's just *not worth it* to chance that. I need to focus on the big picture and my best long-term interests. That means I need to calm down!"

Sometimes it's not an interaction with someone else that sets you off. It can be something as simple and universal as the weather. Let's look at how Kitty salvages her day off, despite the rain, by reasoning with herself.

Scene: Labor Day holiday. It's raining.
Thoughts: It always rains on my day off. I have the rottenest luck. Another vacation ruined. I may as well give up.
Feelings: Disgusted, angry, sad, disappointed

Kitty's aware that these negative thoughts and feelings are really affecting her mood, so she asks her I AM WORTH IT questions.

1. Is it Important? "Yes."

2. Is it Appropriate? "Well, yes and no. It doesn't always rain on my day off. And it's an exaggeration to say the day is ruined. Disgusted and angry seem a little strong, when I think about it. Even sad seems a bit much. But, yes, it's appropriate to be disappointed."

3. Is it Modifiable? "No. I can't stop the rain."

Once she hits a no in the questions, Kitty knows it's time to move on and control her reactions. Now, we know how frustrating the modifiable no can be, but in many ways, it can also be the most liberating. You really have no better choice than to get over whatever it is that's bugging you.

Kitty can begin with self-talk: "I can't make the rain stop, and I also don't want to spend the day getting soaked outside. But I still have the day off, so now I have a chance to think about what I'd most like to do inside. I could get extra sleep. I could invite somebody over. I could read a book or watch the soaps. I could make a batch of fudge.

"My day might not be what I'd hoped for, but it's not ruined."

In helping Kitty to see her other options, this self-talk may help her calm down somewhat. Now it's your turn to practice reasoning with yourself. Look over your Thoughts and Feelings Log and pick out those entries where you got a no to one of the I AM WORTH IT questions. Put yourself back into that situation and try to reason with yourself. We find it's easier to envision this if you imagine yourself as a caring friend or colleague, someone you trust. What would this person say to you if he were trying to convince you not to be upset? Or you can try asking yourself, "Why did I answer no to that question?" You can also frame your questions positively. "What would it be like *not* to feel this way? What else could I accomplish or enjoy if I weren't thinking about this problem right now?" Simple mind shifts can help you see immediate alternatives.

Try to Shut Off Unwanted Thoughts

Even after reasoning with yourself, you may find that you have leftover frustration. This can certainly be a natural reaction, considering that the original situation was so upsetting to begin with. If you're still feeling irritated, thought-stopping can help you get beyond this negative state.

The theory behind thought-stopping is interesting: Some believe that continually dwelling on negative thoughts can become a kind of compulsive behavior. In other words, some people get "hooked" on thinking bad thoughts. If you find this is true for you, try these simple tricks.

"Stop!" yourself. Whenever you find it difficult to stop thinking unwanted thoughts, just tell yourself "Stop!" in a sharp voice. Suppose something has just irritated you. You've gotten a no to one of the I AM WORTH IT questions. Before you spend a lot of time stewing and deliberating on the issue, yell "Stop!" (As this could be awkward in public, and we don't want people to think you're losing it, we recommend that you begin to practice thought-stopping when alone.)

Recall an out-loud shout. Once you've mastered the technique and found it helpful, you can call in reinforcements. If you live with someone, tell your partner about your success with the method and ask for some help. Then choose a time when you're both at home alone. Establish a predetermined signal, and when you become irritated—perhaps at someone on TV or an incorrect bill in the mail—signal your partner to yell at you to "Stop!"

Now, we're not suggesting that you let your partner shout at you continually. Just do this exercise two or three times, at which point you'll have the material you need. You can now move on to the last step: Whenever you need to quit thinking about something, you can recall those shouts. You'll be self-talking as well as remembering how the yell sounded.

Snap yourself. A related approach that some find effective is to keep a loose rubber band around your wrist. When you begin to think about a topic you've decided not to think about, snap the rubber band. The small sting will refocus your attention.[2]

Distract Yourself from Unwanted Thoughts and Feelings

For most of us, agreeable subjects are easier to focus on than disagreeable ones. The trick is to have some subjects at hand so you can immediately substitute the good for the bad.

Start by coming up with a list of topics you like to think about and write it down in your notebook, leaving a blank line or two after each topic. Your list should include whatever will work for you, but here are some favorites:

- A beloved relative
- A good time you had in the past
- A holiday or other family gathering
- A pleasant vacation spot
- An enjoyable sport or activity
- An event you're looking forward to

Now you'll have some topics in reserve, and you can add to them periodically if you want. Use them when you need substitute thoughts for situations in which you've had one or more no answers to the I AM WORTH IT questions.

Next, start at the top of the list and read the first topic, take a deep breath, and close your eyes. Picture that person, place, or experience in your mind. What do you notice right away? Are there any smells or tastes that you associate with this topic? Are there vibrant colors or anything else that you can describe? Open your eyes, and next to that topic, jot down a few expressive words that will later help evoke this image in your mind.

Remember the imagery exercise you learned last week, when you observed how your body reacted when you imagined sitting next to someone you don't like? When you become riled in other situations, your body's responses are likely to be similar. After you use an item from your list to distract yourself, briefly scan your body to sense the moment that you stop reacting this way. Maybe you'll notice that your palms have stopped sweating or your heartbeat has slowed down. Perhaps your face won't feel as flushed.

Practice Relaxation Exercises
Let's say you've tried reasoning with yourself, then yelling "Stop!" You also tried using one of your distractions, but that didn't work. If you're still upset, it's time to calm your body as well as your mind.

Take Harry, for example. Harry worked out at his company's gym four times a week, which helped him to flush out the stress hormones that accumulated during his days as a high-powered sales executive. But whenever an expected sale failed to materialize, he stayed upset and charged up for the rest of the day. Until it was time to hit the gym and sweat out some of that stress, his body remained at the mercy of his negative thoughts. The problem was, Harry's mind was as flabby as his body was taut; he needed to train his mind the same way he had trained his body.

Learning to relax your body is an ability that has benefits for your health beyond the moment in which it is used. Mind-body researchers such as Herbert Benson, MD, founding president of the Mind/Body Medical Institute and associate professor of medicine at Harvard Medical School,[3] and Robert Schneider, MD, director of the Center for Natural Medicine and Prevention,[4] have shown that training people with high blood pressure to relax using meditation-based techniques can reduce blood pressure and even slow arterial damage caused by high blood pressure. Working with relaxation exercises regularly can actually retrain your entire nervous system to stay more tranquil throughout the day.

The 1-minute relaxation exercise. Most people find that this progressive relaxation technique is a relatively easy place to start. The exercise helps train you to coordinate your breathing while relaxing a succession of muscles. Its beauty is that you need only a minute to begin reversing the health-damaging effects of the stress response.

Start by sitting in a chair with both feet on the floor. Read through the exercise a few times until you're familiar with the steps. Then put the book nearby so you can refer to it if you forget a step. Try to breathe evenly and slowly. Close your eyes and begin.

1. Picture a Stop sign and say "Stop" to yourself.

2. Take three slow, deep breaths and say "Relax" as you exhale.

3. Clench your fists while inhaling, then relax them as you exhale.

4. Clench your toes as you inhale and relax them while exhaling.

5. Shrug your shoulders while inhaling, then relax them as you exhale.

6. Inhale while tilting your head to the right, then straighten it while exhaling.

7. Tilt your head to the left as you inhale, then straighten it as you exhale.

8. Inhale, then relax.

9. Open your eyes and take a moment to reorient yourself to your surroundings.

10. Once you have your bearings, go on with your day.

When you have mastered this exercise, you may find that you're able to use it "on the fly" during situations that upset you. If you have just a minute, perhaps you can duck quickly into a bathroom stall or somewhere else where you can close the door. If need be, you can keep your eyes open and practice wherever you are. After you've done the exercise, you're likely to be in a much better frame of mind about the situation that got you riled up in the first place.

Of course, you don't need to wait for a stressful situation to use this exercise. In fact, repeated "preventive" relaxation may help keep upsetting situations from occurring to begin with!

The directed breathing exercise. You may find that once you've mastered the 1-minute relaxation exercise, you want to progress to longer training periods. Initially, Harry wasn't willing to consider any relaxation exercise that lasted more than a minute, because he was skeptical about the benefits. What kind of results can you get from just breathing and clenching? But soon he was hooked, and he realized that these meditative moments could add up to the same kind of personal and physical mastery that he achieved at the gym.

The exercise that he later adopted involved longer periods of breathing and reducing tension in different areas of his body by imagining sending his breath out through that part of his body. He also started using this exercise occasionally while at work.

To begin, read through the exercise, then:

1. Sit in a comfortable position with your legs uncrossed and your hands unclasped. Breathe comfortably and naturally. If possible, close your eyes.

2. As you exhale, think of the number 1 and let yourself feel quite relaxed. Take several breaths, thinking of the number 1 each time you exhale.

3. As you exhale, think of the number 2 and let yourself feel even more relaxed. Take several more breaths, thinking of the number 2 each time you exhale.

4. Exhale and think of the number 3, letting yourself feel very deeply relaxed. Take several breaths, thinking of the number 3 each time you exhale.

5. Next, let yourself imagine that you can send your breath to any part of your body.

6. As you exhale, let the breath flow down your legs, into your feet, and out through your toes. Let your breath take away all the tension in your lower body. Take several breaths, sending your breath out through your toes each time you exhale.

7. As you exhale, let the breath flow down your arms, into your hands, and out through your fingers. Let your breath take away all the tension in your upper body. Take several breaths, sending the breath out through your fingers with each exhalation.

8. On the next exhale, let the breath flow up through your neck and out through your head. Take several breaths, sending the breath out through your head with each exhale.

9. When you feel ready, open your eyes and tell yourself that you feel alert and refreshed.

With practice, the directed breathing exercise can be quite beneficial. Try it any time you have a few minutes of downtime—for example, while traveling on a subway or bus. Once you've gotten the knack of staying focused on your breath, you can call on these exercises whenever a situation upsets you and the one-minute relaxation exercise hasn't been sufficient to get you beyond the crisis. Let us mention, though, that if you wait until a calamitous situation to begin practicing, your powers of concentration probably won't be up to the challenge.

The attention-focusing exercise. When you've mastered the first two exercises, you're ready to move on to this technique, in which you remain exclusively focused on your breath for longer periods of time. This is a discipline that trains your mind to empty itself so your attention can remain focused on something as elemental as your breath. Whenever your attention wanders—and it will—simply return your focus to your breath.

Focusing your attention in this way is one of the most effective means of bringing about a deeply restful state. Research has shown that your body will lower oxygen consumption, decrease heart and respiration rates, and increase the electrical resistance of the skin, suggesting a lowering of anxiety. In fact, while in the attention-focusing state, your body responds much as it does while in the second-deepest level of sleep, when it is just short of dreaming.[5]

Before you start, find a quiet, pleasant place and sit or lie comfortably. Try to select a time and place where you won't be disturbed, no matter what. If you don't live alone, enlist your partner or roommate to ensure that you're not interrupted by phone calls, your children's curiosity, or visits from the family dog.

Set an alarm clock, or ask your partner or roommate to come get you after 15 minutes have passed. If you're sitting, place both feet flat on the floor with your arms at your sides or in your lap. (Avoid a position in which you're likely to fall asleep!) Close your eyes and begin.

1. Focus your attention on your breathing, observing your natural breathing rhythms.

2. See if you can feel the physical sensation of each breath as it passes through your nose or mouth. Does it feel warm or cool? Fast or slow?

3. You may find yourself thinking about something other than the feel of your breath. If this happens (and it probably will), return your focus to the sensation of breathing. Don't judge or tell yourself, "I blew the attention focusing." Just return your attention to your breath.

4. Maintain this focused attention until your predetermined signal brings you out of this state.

Once you learn this attention-focusing exercise, you can do it anywhere, for any length of time. Try it whenever you're riding in a car or bus or while you're waiting for an appointment.

After he tried this exercise, Harry was soon practicing at home about 5 days a week. He decided to do the technique for 15 minutes and set his alarm clock to alert him when the time was up. As he practiced, he found that the length of time between his mental wanderings became longer. To stay focused, Harry found it helpful to add a simple visual image. He decided to picture a wave of water rolling onto the beach when he exhaled, then rolling back out to sea when he inhaled. You can use any simple image that works for you. Some people also add a short favorite saying, such as a line from a poem, a short scripture verse, or just "Calm down" when breathing in and "Smile" when breathing out.

With his meditation practice, Harry's body got even better—on the *inside*. When you meditate on a regular basis, your body reaps many significant long-term benefits: Your heart rate slows; your breathing becomes more regular; and even the number of stress hormones circulating in your bloodstream decreases.

At first, Harry didn't notice much mental difference—but then, he hadn't seen an immediate difference when he first began working out. He continued to practice for 15 minutes a day, 5 days a week. After a month, Harry felt calmer, more grounded, and more centered. Another, unexpected benefit became equally important to him: Whether he was listening to what someone was saying or working alone on a project, he found himself better able to keep his attention focused on what he was supposed to be doing.

Some people find that either the directed breathing exercise or the attention-focusing exercise works better for them. Try both at first, and after a few days, you can decide which is better for you. Once you've made that decision, consider making a commitment to yourself for the next month to reserve a set place and time to practice your chosen exercise. Ask yourself:

- How long is sensible for me?
- Where will I do this?

With this information, write the exercise into your appointment book (in ink) for each day. That way, if you miss one day, you'll be reminded to get back on schedule the next. Plus, you'll be making your own well-being a priority.

JERRY LEARNS TO CHANGE HIS REACTION

Jerry wasn't alone in feeling the crush of job pressure; many of his fellow officers were also suffering because of it. Fortunately, there were some sharp training officers in Jerry's department who were concerned about burnout and health. They instituted our coping-skills training program to help their colleagues deal with trivial as well as major frustrations. The goal was not only to minimize their reactivity to irritations but also to help them develop the capacity to make a graceful transition from being on-duty to being off-duty.

Established police protocols helped Jerry negotiate some of the stickier moments on the job; now he needed an "everything else" protocol. To begin, Jerry practiced what he learned in Weeks 1 and 2 to increase his awareness and then evaluate the situations in which he found himself. Here's a sample log entry.

Scene: *Wednesday, after second shift. Come home to find Kate wearing a top that exposes 2 inches of midriff and a skirt several inches above her knees.*
Thoughts: *What the !*#+*!*
Feelings: *Angry, disgusted, frustrated, disappointed*

Since he was experiencing negative thoughts and feelings, Jerry asked his I AM WORTH IT questions.

1. Is it Important? "Yes."

2. Is it Appropriate? "Maybe my thoughts and feelings are appropriate, maybe not—I'm not sure."

3. Is it Modifiable? "Yes. I could forbid it."

4. Is it **WORTH IT**? "No, not when I consider the needs of everybody involved."

Once he got a no, it was time for him to apply the techniques he learned this week. With his fourth question, Jerry had begun to consider the perspectives of his wife and daughter: "Dora tells me that every little girl in the seventh grade dresses just like Kate. And when I remember times I've seen Kate's classmates, that's true.

Telling Kate she can't dress like that will not only make her resentful, it may even make her a seventh-grade social outcast. Kate is a good kid. I need to focus on that. Plus, Dora and I have enough disagreements as it is without adding the burden of something as petty as this!"

Jerry found that he really liked self-talk. He tried a new tactic: He imagined he was talking to one of his direct reports. He often managed to quiet his responses at work by thinking, "I may be overreacting. At first, I was sure I was in the right, but now I can see that I reacted before considering the situation as a whole." Then he tried it at home. When his son arrived late for dinner one night, Jerry reasoned, "I don't remember if I told Mitch we were having company for dinner. Maybe he did think dinner was at the usual time. Maybe he did need to stay a little after 6:00 to finish helping his friend. Dora and I have preached to him about helping out a buddy whenever you can. When I consider Mitch's perspective, maybe he thought he was doing a good deed."

He even broadened it to long-standing issues that really bothered him: "Look, I can't change that both Dora and I need to work to save money for the kids' education. I can't change that all these damned chores need doing at home. Being greeted by a list of things to do is annoying. But I need to calm down."

By thinking about his self-talk as if he were "supervising" himself to encourage the best possible behavior, Jerry was able to think more rationally and, as a result, more effectively.

When things got a little bit more complex, Jerry moved on to thought-stopping. He found this straightforward enough and even began keeping a loose rubber band around his wrist. When he snapped it, boy, did his brain come to attention!

Jerry made a list of distractions that were likely to succeed, carefully avoiding all references to work, since that was such a major cause of his stress.

- Striped bass I caught on the last fishing trip
- Our next fishing trip
- Whether my team would win the pennant

- Uncle Joseph
- Mitch's home run during the last home game
- Downhill skiing last January

He quickly got the knack of the 1-minute exercise and used it frequently during downtime on duty, but he never got into the habit of the longer meditation. What he did learn, however, suggested that some scheduled transition time when he got home after a shift was a good idea.

The whole family agreed: The first 15 minutes after arriving home became Jerry's "time off" from his family. Dora and the kids were not to confront him with anything then. Instead, he would go into the bedroom and just be by himself. Once he emerged refreshed, he was ready to really be there for his family. Thanks to those 15 minutes, Jerry became a much more tender, open, and playful husband and father—and he also spent a lot less time at the bar after his shifts.

With all of the changes Jerry was making to improve his emotional health, he realized a physical checkup might be in order as well. He made an appointment with his doctor, who ordered a treadmill test. After a few more tests, his doctor diagnosed slightly clogged arteries. Thankfully, they caught it at a stage at which Jerry only needed to take one baby aspirin each day, not a statin drug. His doctor strongly encouraged Jerry to change his diet and begin an exercise program, which he did. Somehow, with life at work and at home improving, these changes seemed easier.

You too can succeed at getting over unwanted negative thoughts and feelings. With practice, these techniques will become not only easier to remember but also less awkward to practice. You don't have to be at the mercy of your first reaction. You can learn to get over it—and your body will thank you!

Week 3 Recap

If you've asked the I AM WORTH IT questions and gotten any no answers, you have a number of tools you can try.

1. Reason with yourself.
2. Say "Stop!" either aloud or silently.
3. Distract yourself by thinking about a favorite topic.
4. Practice the 1-minute relaxation exercise.
5. Practice the directed breathing exercise.
6. Practice the attention-focusing exercise.

CHAPTER 6

WEEK 4: RESOLVE PROBLEMS AND IMPLEMENT SOLUTIONS

You have learned to address only those situations that you have determined are Important to you, Appropriate to be upset about, Modifiable in some way, and **Worth** the effort when all perspectives are considered. Last week, you learned how to damp down overreactions and lingering distress in other situations that did not call for action. This week, you'll learn to think as creatively as you can about potential solutions when the problem is the situation itself. You'll try to solicit suggestions from others whenever possible. You'll also learn to decide on and commit to a course of action, doing whatever is necessary to implement that plan. You may need to make several attempts at a solution, and you may not always succeed in solving every problem. You will, however, be able to control a larger portion of your life by applying this skill.

Tall and broad-shouldered, Harriette Nelson used to be rather good-looking. For the past couple of years, though, she hadn't had much time to take care of herself. Although she would have liked to rinse the gray out of her shiny, chin-length brown hair, of which she'd always been proud, she hesitated because of the time the upkeep would require. Menopause had stuck her with a few more pounds than she would have liked, but who had time to exercise? How could she possibly add one more thing?

"Sandwich generation" wasn't just a phrase to Harriette. She married George when she was in her mid-thirties; their son, Rick, was born when she was 37 and their daughter, Stephanie, 2 years later. The couple lived in Dallas with the children, now 17 and 15.

Harriette's mother lived nearby in a retirement community, where she had moved from Chicago after her husband died. She told anyone who would listen that she had chosen this particular facility so she could be close to Harriette and the grandchildren.

Most days on her way home from work, Harriette stopped by to chat with her mom for a few minutes. They'd talk about the weather and their meals that day. Each time, without fail, Harriette's mother would ask how the children were, but Harriette's answer could easily have been the same each day — by the following afternoon, her mother had forgotten what she'd been told the day before.

Harriette tried to have her mother over to her house at least once each weekend. Mom was glad to eat whatever she made, but if her mom weren't there, Harriette probably wouldn't have done any cooking on the weekend beyond fixing sandwiches. She made the effort because she knew the family dinner was the highlight of the week for her mother.

Add to this mix George's parents, who lived in Waco, about 100 miles away. Both had heart conditions and needed increasing support to be able to stay in their home. George tried to visit at least once a month for the day — more often whenever possible. He did small repairs, took them on errands, and in general tried to keep their increasingly wobbly ship afloat. Because of the distance, taking care of his parents' needs was about all the extra responsibility George could handle, especially since his promotion.

A few months earlier, George had become area manager for a chain of drugstores, which meant long, irregular hours. Before he accepted the promotion, he and Harriette had long discussions about whether he should take the position, given their heavy family responsibilities. Together, they'd concluded they needed the extra money to pay for upcoming education expenses. George would work the longer hours, and Harriette would be in charge of other family duties, such as ferrying

Rick and Stephanie to and from baseball practice, gymnastics, youth group at church, and piano lessons. She had also agreed to help out as much as she could with George's parents.

Harriette enjoyed her job managing the office staff at a research and development center for an international company. She had regular hours, and she was proud that her office ran smoothly, thanks in large part to her organizational efforts over many years. She'd made sure there were manuals and protocols for almost everything. Job descriptions were clear-cut and complete, and workers were trained to cover for one another.

While she'd never had any real downtime at work, she'd become super-busy. As the center had expanded, so had her responsibilities for payroll and bookkeeping for the office staff. What had once been two small tasks had ballooned to occupy significant portions of her workday, on top of everything else.

The office was her exclusive turf, and she was proud that she'd created an operation that could be the envy of many organizations. Her boss often told her she was doing an exceptional job, and each year, she was grateful and gratified by the special birthday celebration given by her staff. She knew they appreciated what a good supervisor she was, and that felt satisfying.

Quitting her job to better deal with the family's needs wasn't feasible. With the kids so near college age, her good salary was necessary to cover the enormous costs. She also knew she wouldn't want to stay home forever—she liked the personal contact and stimulation. Plus, it would take years to achieve this smooth an operation at a new place.

Her frantic schedule left no time for her formerly beloved outings with friends—no lunches, movies, or walks along nature trails. In order to have any time for recreation and socializing, she would have had to give up the precious little downtime she currently had. She needed those brief respites when she didn't have to do anything but sit, instead of being constantly "on." As a result, enjoying regular outings became a thing of the past.

Harriette realized that she was drowning in multiple responsibilities. She knew *she had a very serious problem, but she couldn't see a way out. Formerly in control, she now watched her life getting swept away without her.*

Harriette Needed to Slash Her To-Do List

Up until this point in her life, Harriette had always been able to deal admirably with whatever came along: dealing with an incompetent boss, coping with a difficult first pregnancy, having a toddler and an infant at the same time, helping her mother dismantle the Chicago house and trying to stem the tide of her memory problems, and too much more to even think about. She prided herself on her juggling abilities; now, she reasoned, she'd just have to increase her efforts.

Her children were not as needy as they had been when they were younger, but they still depended on her to help with homework, chauffeur them around, keep a smoothly run household, and especially be there to listen when they wanted to talk. Harriette was gratified that the two kids still talked to her and George—they were teenagers, after all. Her son and daughter were good kids: They tried hard, got admirable grades in school, and had a number of friends. They were turning out well, and Harriette knew it was important that she continue to be involved in their lives.

When she looked at the situation with her mother, Harriette saw herself as her mom's only real human contact. Mom needed Harriette to stop by every day and invite her over on the weekends—she really didn't have anyone else to turn to. Neither did George's parents. Harriette wanted to be there for them, just as she hoped their children would be if she and George ever needed them.

Working also took energy. When she thought about George's promotion, she could see how logical it had been for him to accept it, even though that decision had increased her own burden.

Taken one at a time, each of these demanding situations seemed to have only one commonsense solution: Let Harriette do it! But as Harriette's log entries testify, her problem was clear: She simply had too much to do, with no time for herself.

To add insult to injury, Harriette had nightly hot flashes that robbed her of

Harriette's Log

Scene: *Monday morning. Beginning the week tired. Woke up twice last night with hot flashes. George asks me if I can drop off his jacket at the dry cleaners on the way to work.*

Thoughts: *Can't anyone else in this family ever be responsible for anything? I know George has to get to work sooner than I do. And he's been putting in a lot of hours recently. But so have I.*

Feelings: *Frustrated, discouraged*

Behavior: *Tell him I'll do it.*

Consequences: *Ten minutes late getting to work. Make up the time with a shorter lunch break. Feel less on top of things by the end of the day.*

Scene: *Need to do about 45 minutes of grocery shopping on the way home. Mother calls to ask if I can take her by the church to drop off her contribution to tomorrow's bazaar.*

Thoughts: *Why couldn't she tell me this last weekend? Her memory seems to be getting worse. It will be good for her to be thanked in person, but I don't need this today. It'll be 7 o'clock by the time I get home. Maybe I'll purchase roasted chickens at the store. The roads and the grocery store are going to be even more crowded at 6:00 than at 5:30.*

Feelings: *Irritated, frustrated, tired*

Behavior: *Tell Mother I'll be there. Slip out of work 15 minutes early.*

Consequences: *Mother's errand takes a half hour from pickup to return. She seems grateful I took her. Grocery store then takes longer. Get home by 7:30. Family hungry and irritable. I'm irritable, too.*

much-needed sleep. At a time in her life when it would have been self-nurturing to devote more attention to herself, she was having to do the opposite.

Slowly and inexorably, Harriette was becoming overwhelmed. More often than before, she was grouchy with the very people she most wanted to treat well.

DEAL WITH IT

Like Harriette, at some point in our lives, we all feel the crush of having a lot—even too much—to deal with. While day-to-day living can feel like just enough, an illness in the family or a broken leg can push us to the brink.

Consider what happens when your car breaks down. Even if it's a second car and not that new, you have to decide if fixing it would cost more than it's worth. Springing for a new car would be quite expensive, but another piece of junk would probably be a bad investment.

Or perhaps you deserved a promotion, but someone else got it. Now you have to figure out what you want your future career path to be—stay at this job, move on, or switch gears altogether?

In the United States today, 70 percent of working people don't think there's a healthy balance between their work and their personal lives. Forty-six percent feel either overworked, overwhelmed by the quantity of their work, or lacking the time to step back and reflect on their work.[1] Chances are, you're among them.

Every day, we're faced with countless choices and tradeoffs. Often, we make these choices unconsciously because the right path is so obvious. Sometimes, though, we see no solution to one or more problems. We may reach a crisis point. Something has to give, but it's often not clear what, when, or how.

At home, many of us lack the resources to carve out the time we need to feel a sense of control over our lives, let alone peace and balance. The number of families headed by single mothers has increased by about 25 percent over the past 10 years, and single-father households have tripled in the past couple of decades. Perhaps your situation is similar. Forget contentment, you may be thinking—I'd be happy with 10 minutes alone!

Week 4 isn't going to make these or other difficult situations vanish. Problems arise every day, and having control means that you're able to deal with them—as opposed to avoiding them in the first place. In today's world, sometimes even a partial solution can be a big help. But first, you need to spend some energy deciding which problems to focus on.

Before launching into a problem-solving session, take the time to ask yourself the four I AM WORTH IT questions. That way, you're not focusing on a matter that's unimportant or that has more to do with your reactions than with the situation itself. Remember, not all problems are solvable, but it's always useful to double-check that you're being very honest with yourself, just to be sure you're not merely giving up.

When you're faced with a problem, ask yourself the four questions. If you get any no answers, you know it's time to use the skills you'll learn in Week 3. You then know to stop reacting to what shouldn't or can't be changed. You have better things to do with your time.

On the other hand, if a predicament should be solved and it may be possible to do it, your imagination can run free and devise a way out of at least part of your difficult situation. You can then focus your energy on that, as Alfred did.

Alfred was in his thirties and married, with two kids. His job was measuring air quality for a large government agency, monitoring pollutants to be sure they didn't exceed the legal limit. He loved his job but needed a promotion in order for the family to be able to stop worrying about finances. .

When the family's second car stopped running, Alfred found himself at a loss. He was upset, and he knew he needed a solution to his problems. First, he wrote this log entry.

Scene: Car quit while I was driving it. Had it towed to the repair shop. Spent $75 right there. They told me it would cost $2,000 to get it running again. Based on the description of what was wrong, a second estimate was even higher.

Thoughts: It's not worth much more than that! What will go next? And it's wasted money to buy another jalopy. But I need my car to get to work. I won't make it to work on time ever again. I won't be able to keep my flexible schedule. I'm going to lose my chance for promotion. This isn't fair, when I work so hard. I need that promotion. Nothing ever works out for me. I need reliable transportation, but I also need to stay out of debt and save money for a down payment on a house.

Feelings: Angry, sad, disgusted, worried, afraid

Because he had these negative thoughts and feelings, Alfred asked himself the I AM WORTH IT questions.

1. Is it Important that my car won't run and I don't want to spend the money necessary to fix it? "Yes!"

2. Is it Appropriate to be angry, sad, disgusted, worried, and afraid? "I think so."

Is it appropriate to think that I'm going to have to give up my flexible schedule? "Maybe yes, maybe no."

Is it appropriate to think that nothing ever works out for me? "Not really. I have a satisfying job and a great family. That's a lot right there. On the other hand, it is appropriate to think this isn't fair, when I work so hard."

Is it appropriate for me to worry about money? "Yes—I'm right that I need to stay out of debt and save money for a down payment on a house."

3. Is there anything I can do to Modify this situation? "I can't change the fact that my car won't run. But I should be able to find a way to get to work—and possibly still stay on a flexible schedule."

4. Would it be **WORTH IT** to try? "Absolutely! Besides, having adequate transportation could help ensure that I get that important promotion."

Once Alfred had four yes answers, he knew he needed to try to change the situation. He could see clearly that it wasn't the behavior of another person that was creating the problem. The real problem was that he needed a way to get to work—and that might be a problem he could solve.

Effective problem solving involves seven actions.

1. Define the problem.

2. Clarify your goals and objectives.

3. List all possible solutions.

4. Make a decision.

5. Implement the decision.

6. Evaluate the outcome.

7. Reconsider options as necessary.

Define the Problem

You can see what's bothering you, so why not dive right into solving it? Because you don't have limitless energy and you need to strategize—that's why. You need to begin by clarifying the issue in very exact terms.

Sometimes the problem is limited to one specific occasion. One way you'll know this is the case is when the "scene" section of your log entries shows something unusual: a canceled flight, power knocked out by an ice storm, a highway reduced to two lanes for a day. Other times, it's a cumulative problem shown by a number of similar log entries: not enough time for yourself, more bills than money to pay them, a child's homework consistently not getting done, a diet not resulting in weight loss.

Take a look through your Thoughts and Feelings Log entries thus far and pick a situation that jumps out at you. You can use either one of your original entries or one that you've written since then. If you haven't already, ask yourself the I AM WORTH IT questions. If you have four yes answers, and the problem is the situation itself, can you clearly articulate what the problem is?

Once you think you've isolated the problem, make sure you can answer one of these two questions. First question: "What is it I have that I don't want? (Some answers might be "I'm carpooling my daughter to early swim practice every morning, Monday-Friday," "The work of the ethics committee no longer interests me," "The cedars planted across the front of our house are too overgrown to just trim back," "Smoking has become for me an addiction.") Second question: "What is it I don't have that I do want?" (Some answers might be "Another way to reach my destination," "The best way to cope with the loss of electricity," "A good alternate route on Monday," "More time to myself," "A means of dealing with too many bills," "A plan for getting my child to complete homework assignments," "A weight-loss plan that works.")

Now, write your problem at the top of a page in your notebook. Use definitive language: "I don't have enough time to myself" or "Jimmy won't sit down to do his homework." Be sure to do this; otherwise, as you move through the process, the topic may slip over from one subject onto a related but not identical subject. Pinning down the issue gets you that much closer to a resolution.

The description of the scene gave Alfred a definition of his problem: "I don't want to spend the money to get my car fixed, but I've got to get to work, preferably on a flexible schedule."

Clarify Your Goals and Objectives

You need to be clear about where you want the focus to be. We have found this really helps to concentrate energies productively. "I want Mary to get in trouble for this" may give way to "I want Mary to let the boss know I was responsible for creating The Jones Project Report." Ask yourself, "What do I want most in this situation?"

List All Possible Solutions

Here's the really fun part. For the moment, live in a fantasy world of limitless possibilities: What would be your ideal solutions? Consider all the options, even the crazy ones, and write them down. Sometimes the kernel of a great idea is contained in a seemingly impractical thought.

Alfred knew that he needed some help in coming up with new ideas. He'd been thinking about his transportation problems for so long that he was having a hard time getting a fresh perspective. He decided to ask his golfing buddies for help. As they played one Saturday morning, Alfred and his friends brainstormed as they moved from hole to hole. Alfred had set the ground rules: There's no such thing as a bad idea, no matter how crazy it sounds. He was just looking for *volume* of ideas at this point.

His friends took up the challenge, and Alfred scribbled furiously on the back of his scorecard as they shouted out one idea after another. Here's the list they came up with.

- Walk to the bus stop five blocks away and take the bus.
- Quit my job.
- Ask a co-worker who lives nearby for a ride as a favor.
- Pay that co-worker to give me a ride.
- Borrow my mom's car until I can afford a good replacement.
- Try to get a friend to fix my car for the cost of parts.
- Ride a bike to work (5 miles away).
- Get a loan from the bank.
- Rob a bank.
- Ask my uncle for a loan.
- Get an extra job.

Once you've finished this chapter, assemble a group who can act as your own personal think tank. Try to invite people you consider to be naturally positive and energetic, who see the glass as half full and can make a brainstorming exercise fun. Often brainstorming sessions are the most productive if they're spontaneous, such as when you're at a dinner party with a lot of smart people or shopping with or eating lunch with friends. But if you have time to arrange a brainstorming session, ask yourself what you can do to ensure that your helpers will have a good time. Be sure they're well fed and having fun so they'll be happier and more helpful to you. If you have the room and access to a flipchart, you can use that to record the suggestions, and be sure to copy all the results into your notebook.

Remember, before you ask others to help, be sure you have the problem you most want to work on clearly in mind so you can articulate it to your friends. And while brainstorming works better with several people providing input, you can generate suggestions on your own if necessary.

Make a Decision

While generating ideas is important—and can be very enjoyable—in order to truly solve your problem, you need to move from thinking to doing. Many people find that making plans and setting goals can be energizing; after feeling powerless over your problems, you finally have a plan that can put you back in control.

First, quickly go through your list and cross out any options that aren't plausible, such as "win the lottery." These may have been fun to consider and freed your imagination. Still, crazy options are the ones over which you're not likely to have much control or that have a large downside.

Next, if you have enough remaining options, group similar ones together. They may overlap or combine into a better solution.

Finally, look at each of the remaining suggestions, pick the one or two that seem the most reasonable, and write down the answers to the following questions:

- Exactly what needs to be done to make this work?

- Can it be stated in terms of one overall action, or does it have to be broken down into smaller actions?

- Who is going to be responsible for each part of whatever action is decided upon?

- When is each of these actions going to be evaluated to see if the problem has been solved? What will be the benchmarks of the evaluation? What will be the timetable?

Alfred went through the list he had jotted down on the back of his scorecard. He crossed out all the possible solutions that wouldn't work for sure or were likely to have terrible outcomes.

- Take the bus.
- ~~Quit my job.~~
- Ask a co-worker for a ride as a favor.
- Pay that co-worker to give me a ride.
- Borrow my mom's car.
- Try to get a friend to fix my car.
- Ride a bike to work.
- Get a loan from the bank.
- ~~Rob a bank.~~
- Ask my uncle for a loan.
- Get an extra job.

Alfred then asked his friends if they thought any ideas could be combined. They decided that yes, several fit very nicely together.

- *Get others to help:* Ask a co-worker for a ride as a favor, pay the co-worker for a ride, borrow my mom's car, get a friend to fix my car.
- *Get some money:* Get a loan from the bank, ask my uncle for a loan, get an extra job.
- *Find other transportation:* Take the bus, ride a bike to work.

Alfred then had to choose: What were his one or two best options? Being an independent person, he decided to first try finding other transportation on his own. He already had a bicycle, so his plan was to try that solution for a month, then reevaluate.

He knew that riding his bike had its own set of challenges that might conflict with his ultimate goal of getting the promotion, so he set up a couple of evaluative benchmarks to help him decide if this solution was working. In a month, he would ask himself:

- Am I getting to work on time?
- Do I still have a flexible schedule?
- Do I really enjoy riding my bike?

These questions got at the heart of the bike-riding solution and helped Alfred focus on the real reasons that he chose this option. Moreover, they freed him to change course if the solution wasn't working, before he got to the crisis point again.

Implement the Decision

This is the first moment of the rest of your life. You've clarified the issue, made the plan, and now you'll draw on your determination and drive to solve the problem. You've taken all the guesswork and anxiety out of the picture. Instead of wondering, "How am I going to change this?" you have a plan. In the best of ways, you're just following orders, sir.

If your goal is big and your ultimate solution is a multistep process, make sure you've broken it down into smaller parts that will be easier and less overwhelming to accomplish one at a time. Track all your goals and target dates in your notebook, and be sure to reward yourself by adding a checkmark or other reinforcing sign that you've accomplished your goals.

In Alfred's case, all he needed to do was pump a little more air into his bicycle tires and begin pedaling. Luckily, there were showers at work, so he packed a towel, washcloth, and clean shirt in his backpack so he could freshen up if needed.

Evaluate the Outcome

Part of success is *acknowledging* when you've succeeded. But sometimes, when we've made gains, our evaluation of those gains can be influenced by outside events, our moods, or even the stock market.

Instead of leaving your declaration of victory to the fickle hands of fate, set a date to evaluate your solution and write it down in your notebook when you're detailing the specifics of your plan and how it will be evaluated. Then, on that date, use the predetermined objective criteria to measure your progress. If your plan has succeeded, declare a triumph. For example, maybe Alfred is happy with his solution. The exercise he gets from riding his bicycle is a big plus, and he's happy that he can continue to save money for the future.

On the other hand, your solution may be only partially successful. Perhaps Alfred will say to himself, "I don't mind anything else, but I hate the fumes from cars on the road, and riding in the rain is no picnic." If this is the case, he'll need to make a decision about whether to continue on his present course.

This is a great time to use your thoughts and especially your feelings as a guide. If the thoughts or feelings about your solution are negative, ask the I AM WORTH IT questions to help you decide whether to stick with what you're doing or try something different. Alfred may decide that the negative aspects of riding his bike are important, his reaction is appropriate, and he could modify the situation by trying something different—but given the benefits of the extra exercise and the money he's saving, it's not worth it to try another solution. On the other hand, if Alfred got four yes answers to the questions, he would need to move on and reconsider the options.

We advise you to stay open. Reconsidering your options is not an admission of failure; in fact, it's a clear signal that you're approaching your problems from a pragmatic, solution-oriented perspective.

Reconsider Options as Necessary

You've held onto your original brainstorming list, so go back and check there first. See anything good? Maybe what you thought would never work the first time is more plausible now. If so, make your plan, set a date for reevaluation, and dig in!

If you don't find anything—and we know this can be disheartening—stay positive. You just need to do an abbreviated spin through the problem-solving tactics again.

- Do your brainstorming again. Maybe another solution will occur to you. If so, follow the rest of the process just as you did before.

- If that doesn't work, ask yourself if the problem is different than you thought. If so, go back to defining the problem itself.

- If that doesn't help, you may have to go back to your original I AM WORTH IT questions. Consider the possibility that the situation *isn't* modifiable. Since the circumstances can't be changed, it's better to try to get beyond your unwanted negative thoughts and feelings. When you've reached that conclusion, go back to the deflecting skills you learned last week.

When Alfred hits his 1-month reevaluation point, he may decide to continue riding his bike so he can save money to buy a better car. But if that solution doesn't suit him, he can look back at his original list and see that he still has plenty of other potentially good answers to his problem. He can choose another solution and set another action plan and evaluation date.

Perhaps the most important lesson to learn this week is the knowledge that even when unfortunate things happen, you aren't completely without the resources to deal with them. Alfred's situation was not good, but problem solving helped him realize that it wasn't hopeless. With that insight, Alfred realized that he was less angry, sad, disgusted, and worried.

If you find that you've reached an evaluation date with a happy conclusion, give yourself a treat—look back at your original Thoughts and Feelings Log, the one that prompted the need to solve a problem. We're willing to bet that your emotions will be a darn sight more positive now than they were before you gave yourself the power to change your own life.

HARRIETTE LEARNS TO USE PROBLEM SOLVING

Trapped in a situation that didn't seem to have any solutions, Harriette was drowning in obligations, to-do lists, and guilt. Her responsibilities were important, but she knew she couldn't keep up this schedule for very long without it having serious ramifications for her relationships. How could she get out from under?

She began by sorting out those aspects of the demands on her that got four yes answers to the I AM WORTH IT questions.

- *Responsibilities to her husband and children: four yeses*

- *Responsibilities to her mother: four yeses*

- *Responsibilities to work: four yeses*

- *Responsibilities to herself (meeting personal needs): four yeses*

Clearly, everything was important, but something had to give. (While her responsibilities to George's parents were also important, she decided that they weren't modifiable. And even if they were, it wouldn't be worth it to change them.) Harriette defined her overload as the problem: "I have too many responsibilities."

After explaining to her children and George that her current duties were too much, Harriette scheduled a family brainstorming session. She set out some snacks, explained the rules, and hoped for the best.

Harriette shared her list of responsibilities she had written in her notebook,

- *Transporting Rick and Stephanie to activities*
- *Grocery shopping*
- *Dinner*
- *Laundry*
- *Housecleaning*
- *Help with homework*

Once the group was satisfied that all of Harriette's home tasks were included, they moved on to their ideas for solutions. Everyone shouted out their ideal suggestions.

- *Rick and Stephanie take turns preparing dinner.*
- *Rick and Stephanie take turns doing laundry.*
- *Buy another car so Rick could transport himself and Stephanie to activities.*
- *Hire a full-time housekeeper.*
- *Hire a cleaning service.*
- *Ditch the homework help.*
- *Have more takeout meals, such as pizza one night a week.*
- *Have Rick quit his after-school job so he could help more at home.*

Rick and Stephanie liked the idea of an extra car, and Rick was happy to consider quitting his job, especially if his allowance could be increased. George and Harriette were delighted with the idea of the teenagers taking on more household responsibilities. Everyone agreed that homework help just had to happen. In fact, what made this meeting such a success was the family's larger realization that they weren't just helping Harriette—they were dealing with a problem that involved all of them.

Their final solutions: George and Harriette would get another car and let Rick quit his part-time job, with some increase in his allowance. In turn, Rick would transport Stephanie everywhere she needed to go; once she got her license, they would share the car. In exchange for their car, Rick or Stephanie would begin preparing dinner on nights they didn't order takeout. They would also do the laundry.

Wistfully, Harriette had to admit that a full-time housekeeper was too expensive, but the family convinced her that the occasional use of a cleaning service was affordable. Everyone liked the idea of having takeout food on some nights.

And so it went for the rest of that afternoon and on another occasion. They tackled the list as a team and kept coming up with more and better solutions. For example, they decided that the family members would take turns visiting Harriette's mother, and sometimes they would take her out for dinner instead of inviting her to their house. That meant less work and more entertainment for everyone.

After Stephanie heard her mom's comments about not being able to take care of some of her own needs, she volunteered to help Harriette put a semi-permanent rinse on her hair to give it some highlights. An exercise program was a good idea, so Harriette decided to take brisk walks in the evening when she got home early enough, plus longer walks on the weekends. Outings with friends would have to wait—but just for a little while.

Harriette felt energized. She still would have too much to do, but her situation no longer felt desperate. Laying out plans of action increased her sense of control.

At work, Harriette and her supervisors were able to figure out a couple of ways to delegate some of her responsibilities. The company hired a payroll service, and an accounting firm provided part-time services. Harriette's feeling of being in a blender, whirling at breakneck speed, was diminishing every day.

Still, following through on so many good ideas was a challenge. A reasonably priced car was quickly purchased, and, even more quickly, Rick quit his part-time job. Takeout meals and the occasional cleaning help were great successes. Although having Rick and Stephanie start dinner and do laundry began well, soon George and Harriette had to remind them. This quandary led to another problem-solving session and some modifications to the original plan.

Life was much better for the next 6 months. Harriette felt upbeat and ener-

getic for the first time in years. Since then, she and her family have encountered some serious challenges—Harriette was diagnosed with an early stage of breast cancer—so they were back in a situation of great demands and limited resources. But now they have a system in place. They know they can deal with problems as they arise to make tough situations more bearable for everyone. They also know they work best as a team.

Week 4 Recap

1. When you're aware of negative thoughts and feelings, ask the four I AM WORTH IT questions.

2. If you get four yeses, determine if it's the situation itself that's the problem.

3. If it is, address it on your own or with others.
   - Define the problem.
   - Clarify your goals and objectives.
   - List all possible solutions.
   - Make a decision.
   - Implement the decision.
   - Evaluate the outcome.
   - Reconsider options as necessary.

CHAPTER 7

WEEK 5: ASSERT YOURSELF AND LEARN TO SAY NO

In previous weeks, you learned to be aware of how you think and feel, and how to make decisions about whether or not to act on your feelings. You're probably getting much clearer about what you need. This week, you'll learn to approach matters head-on and ask other people for what you want. This assertiveness will in turn teach you to say no when you need to—keeping your life in balance and enabling you to portion out your time, money, and name according to your own priorities.

While Redford had all the earmarks of a volatile volcano, Virginia spent the first few years of the marriage trying to avoid conflict and sulking after Redford's outbursts. Gradually, as mentioned in Chapter 4, we both began to see that this wasn't serving the relationship well. As we developed our program, Virginia decided that Redford wasn't the only one who needed to make some changes. To help make the marriage successful, she needed to develop the ability to get her needs met without feeling sorry for herself. Here's Virginia's story, in her own words.

Years before I was born, my parents had worked out the protocol for most day-to-day decisions: My mother took the lead, and my father would accommodate. I was greatly influenced by my father, a tall, broad-shouldered, dark-haired man who was exceptionally generous in his dealings with everyone. This was especially true with his family. When he got home from work, he often played catch with me, and he listened with interest to whatever I said, looking for opportunities to praise. (This included sitting through whole piano recitals, although he couldn't even carry a tune except for "Maryland, My Maryland.") I adored him.

I could see that almost everyone in our Tidewater, Virginia, community also respected him. Our next-door neighbor often said, "He's like a father to me." At church, he was the one who usually received the plates after the ushers had finished collecting the offering. When I went out on first dates, the boys would tell me how their fathers had said, "Now, you treat her well!" when they learned who their sons were going out with. His influence even improved my dating life!

I also watched my father constantly accommodate my mother's wishes. He'd say, "Sure, if you want to get there a half hour early, we can leave now," even when there was no earthly reason to be there that early.

I particularly remember one snowy day. I was supposed to go to a dance that night, and my cloth shoes had been sent 20 miles away to be dyed to match my evening dress. At my mom's request, my dad had gone out in the snow to pick up the shoes—not a good idea. (People outside the South may not fully appreciate how little experience most eastern Virginia drivers have with winter road conditions.) Although I had some silver shoes I could have worn, the green shoes were in my closet before lunchtime.

My mom gave my sister and me a lot of attention, too. Even when it involved personal sacrifice, she insisted on the finest of everything for us. When we were young, she read to us every afternoon and often planned interesting new activities for us. One summer afternoon, she showed me how to make "movies" with two sticks, a roll of paper, colored pencils, and a shoebox. This intense involvement carried over into decision making. From her perspective, she had her daughters' best interests in mind, so it was only logical that she be the decision maker.

I started out with a mind of my own. As I grew older, I began to state what I wanted, whether it was to not eat my lima beans, to practice the piano after playing outside first, or to not wear that yucky dress to church. This led to a lot of arguing. Disagreements became constant and contentious during my teenage years. Was it *right for my mom to insist that I wear my black-and-white saddle oxfords with those dumb little buckles in back? Why couldn't I wear the much more fashionable loafers? The battles raged on.*

At 18, I went off to college, feeling that now I could make most of my own decisions. Sometimes I was happy, sometimes unhappy, but at least I felt in charge.

Three days after my 23rd birthday, I married Redford and once again found someone else calling the shots. Embodying the traditional Southern ideal of deference, wives were discouraged from experiencing anger and other negative feelings. By behaving "graciously," a wife set the tone for a happy marriage and, by extension, a happy home.

You've already learned about the meals and other manifestations of housewifery that Redford found less than perfect. At first, I was aware of being hurt in these moments, but not angry. Instead, I pledged to myself that I would redouble my efforts — I would make it right. In reality, though, I wasn't standing up for myself.

Virginia Needed to Stop Moping and Assert Herself

I've always faced a couple of big challenges. I have trouble getting in touch with negative feelings when those feelings are directed toward someone close to me. It can take me a long time to figure out that I'm being treated in ways I dislike. Instead, I accept the dictums of significant others about what I should do, and I tend to accept their criticisms without question, too.

In the first years of our marriage, this situation was especially pronounced. Redford told me I didn't know how to cook a number of different dishes very well. According to him, I also didn't know which movie would be best to see, and I wasn't as good at driving as he was.

While I was hurt, I was not aware of being angry. Redford pronounced, and I believed him. "He thinks my cake isn't chocolate enough — I must have chosen a bad recipe," I'd think. Or, "Well, I guess I drive more slowly because I haven't had a lot of experience on interstates."

Even when I was aware of negative feelings, my first impulse was to sulk and pout rather than ask for a change in behavior. Of course, these suppressed feelings added up, and eventually, once they had reached an intolerable threshold, I would burst out with a litany of how I had been wronged: "You didn't clear your papers off the coffee table as I asked you to last Sunday, so I had to clear them off myself. The table was loaded down again the next day and the next. And now you've messed it up again. You never do your part. This is really unfair!"

Early on, I also had little say in decision making. Redford was adamant that buying an expensive camera was a great investment, so we purchased the camera. Since he had never had a dog as a boy, we should get the Doberman pinscher he wanted instead of the whippet I wanted. Playing bridge with the guys on a Friday night when he wasn't on call at the hospital was more important than shopping for baby clothes. A later shopping excursion found me sulking and Redford looking uninterested.

And so it went, for over a decade. I refined my tendency to pout and sulk. I began to keep a running tab of resentments, and the list grew ever longer. Gradually, I became primed to notice what I considered to be the slightest misbehavior. This marriage was no longer made in heaven!

Whether or not I was conscious of it, on some level, I was presumably experiencing negative feelings on each occasion. I've since learned that researchers have measured the bodily responses of people who are suppressors (or stuffers). When these subjects talk about difficult personal situations or watch upsetting videos, their bodies respond, even though they may not be consciously aware of their negative feelings.

I needed to become aware of negative thoughts and feelings early on and then really master the skill of assertion. If Redford was dishing out inconsiderate treatment, I was spooning it up. Although his role is easier to see at first glance, a closer look reveals that both of us were locked into this pattern of behavior. I could probably have put a stop to it earlier by practicing assertion.

GO FOR IT

In a world of never-ending conflict, getting to a mutually beneficial resolution is often a matter of diplomacy and tact. Different negotiating styles abound, and people often mistakenly believe there are only two options: passively allowing everyone to run roughshod over them or insisting on total dominance.

The mistake of being too passive. Nonassertive people easily fall into feeling victimized. "If the people around me would just behave better, how wonderful life could be," they tend to think. In fact, they need to assume responsibility for being timid, overly accommodating, and "too nice" either in one area or many areas of their lives. As we've seen with Virginia and with Merrison (in Week 1), until they respond more actively to events in their own lives, they're not likely to get the lives they want. Still, in many ways, their inability to stand up for themselves isn't as dangerous as the tendency of their polar opposites to mow everyone down in the process of getting what they want.

The mistake of being too aggressive. At the opposite extreme are people who respond aggressively when provoked.

Don is a perfect example. He often says things like:

- "My mailing needs to go out before that."
- "Eric needs to give priority to my project."
- "No, no, that's not right. Power transistors are the only way to go."
- "The movie I suggested would be a lot better."
- "We need to stay home for the holidays, period."
- "No, you're coming with us, and that's it."

Don always presses forward toward whatever he wants, no matter what. Others either dismiss him quickly or smolder in resentment. There goes Don again, charging forward like a bulldozer! Legitimate needs are surrounded by instances of "me first, whatever the circumstances." If Don actually needed help, chances are nobody would notice. He also finds that few friends or family members truly adore him, so he feels isolated some of the time.

Occasionally, aggression gets results, but not often. The personal relationships of aggressors are usually rocky, and the people around them are usually unhappy. In their rise to positions of leadership at their jobs, aggressors derail at the level of middle manager because they can't motivate their teams. Other damages abound. Exposure to heavy traffic increases risk of a heart attack[1,] but the potential for injury doesn't stop there. In a recent 7-year period, aggressive drivers were responsible for 13,000 people being injured or killed.[2] Another study found that a large number of damaged computer keyboards, shattered monitors, broken mice, and kicked-in hard drives were victims of corporate managerial rage.[3]

In Chapter 1, you learned that aggression takes a toll on the body of the aggressor. "Letting it all out" harms everyone else, too.

To make matters worse, acting aggressively doesn't even get rid of anger, and it may actually make it worse. In one study, psychologists told one group of undergraduates that venting anger is helpful and told another that it's harmful. The belief that it was helpful actually reinforced the desire to express that anger physically.

In a second study, a group of subjects were deliberately angered, and some were given an opportunity to hit a punching bag. Then all of the participants were given a chance to deliver what they thought were painfully loud noises to other people. Some subjects were told that they'd deliver a loud noise to the person who had angered them; others were told the loud noise would be delivered to a third party. In both cases, those who hit the punching bag delivered a more noxious noise — even when the recipient was an innocent bystander! This research clearly points to the conclusion that aggressive behavior actually leads to further expressions of aggression.[4]

Now that you know the twin pitfalls of nonexistent or weak responses and aggressive responses, you can redirect your energies toward a healthy middle ground: assertion. In assertion, you focus on getting the other person to change behavior. Almost all of us can fall into a losing pattern occasionally, but whether you're feeling like a wimp or an aggressor, an assertion booster shot is in order!

Know Your Weaker Areas

Do you have to work very hard to get in touch with negative thoughts and feelings? Perhaps you don't realize that you're upset until long after the fact. If this is the case, you need to spend a lot of time focusing on becoming aware of your feelings. If you tend to be timid and accommodating, three of the I AM WORTH IT questions can be problematic.

1. Is this matter Important? Suppressors have a tendency to answer no. If you're still thinking about the issue after a few hours—and certainly after a few days—revisit the question. You may have to work hard at believing negative situations might really be major. Often, they are minor, but don't you ever deserve to leave first, have the bigger slice of pie, speak first, or get more airtime?

2. Is what I am thinking and/or feeling Appropriate? We've seen many accommodating people flounder on this one because their self-judgments tend to be harsh. Try asking yourself, "If a friend or relative came to me with this situation, described thoughts or feelings similar to ones I'm having, and asked, 'Was I right to be so upset?' what would I say?"

3. Is taking action WORTH IT? The last potential derailment comes in balancing your needs and those of others. Overly accommodating people can dismiss their own needs too easily. Once again, imagine a friend is asking the question. What would you say?

If you usually answer no or usually answer yes, ponder your responses carefully. Perhaps considering the matter afresh may lead to some rethinking. As a second check, describe the situation to someone you respect and ask how that person would have reacted to the four questions. If any answer is different from your own, you may want to deliberate a bit longer before accepting your original response as final.

When the Situation Warrants, Ask for Different Behavior

Troublesome situations don't always involve another person. If your car is almost out of gas, or the babysitter didn't show up and you need to keep an important appointment, you have to solve the problem, period. You'll need to define the problem, brainstorm solutions, and choose and implement your best option.

More often, however, it's someone else's behavior that upsets us, and what we need to do is ask the other person to change that behavior. You want that person to either behave in some good new ways or stop behaving in some bad old ways. And, yes, we're quite aware that this is easier said than done! That's why we devised Week 5's exercises.

Asking for a change in behavior can often be a delicate matter because it's usually in your best interest to accomplish this without offending the other person, if possible. If you manage to be diplomatic, the other person will feel better and be more inclined to cooperate. By not escalating the situation into an angry exchange, you're also less likely to send your body into overdrive in the harmful ways described in the first chapter. Even better, you're more likely to be able to work well with the person in the future.

Assertion always involves making a request. Several kinds of requests are possible.

- *You can ask someone to change his behavior:* "Please clean up the conference room after your meeting."

- *You can ask for more information or clarification:* "Please explain why Catherine was chosen instead of me for the promotion."

- *You can ask to be listened to:* "Will you meet with me this afternoon at 2:30 so I can explain my point of view?"

Always have a clear picture of the *precise* behavior you want from the other person. Remember: When you record the scene in your log entries, you include only what you can see and hear, and you need to be equally objective and precise in thinking about how you want the other person to behave.

"Please be more considerate!" or "Don't be so rude!" isn't specific enough. In return, you may hear, "But I am being considerate," which puts you into a corner. What *exactly* do you want the other person to do or stop doing?

Sometimes a simple request is all that's needed. "Let me finish what I'm saying, please," is an assertive response to being interrupted.

Let's take another example: Jean's daughter and her friend Jessica need rides home from gymnastics practice every Wednesday and Friday night. Jessica's mom has assigned Jean all the Friday night pickups and taken Wednesdays for herself, but Jean prefers Wednesday, too. So she says, "Let's alternate weeks," and Jessica's mom agrees immediately. (She must have known she had the better part of the deal!) By asking for a specific behavior, Jean avoided making an attack such as "That's not fair!" or asking for a vague change in attitude such as "Please be more considerate."

Prepare Well for Your Requests

Ask and ye shall receive—but not before doing a little extra homework. In most cases, complex emotions are involved, so you'll need to complete a few more steps before you make your request. A fully developed request involves two to six steps.

1. Report the situation causing your negative thoughts and/or feelings. We all view our lives through the prism of our own perceptions. You can't assume that someone else will have seen and heard what you did, and you certainly can't expect someone else to know your thoughts and feelings until you report them. Except in the cases of simple requests, if you just launch into a demand for an entirely different behavior out of the blue, you're much less likely to get what you want, because the person has no idea *why* you want this. He has no frame of reference, no history, and consequently, no investment in agreeing. Remember, he's been living in his world, not yours.

Just describe objectively, in a sentence or two, the *specific behavior* that caused your negative feelings. What did the person do or say? Just as you do when you write log entries, focus on the situation that just occurred, not on past events.

Let's say you're on a diet. Your partner has agreed not to eat fattening foods in front of you. One night, he saunters into the room eating an ice cream sundae with hot fudge sauce, walnuts, and whipped cream. He then plops down in his chair, sundae in one hand, spoon in the other.

For now, just keep the exact situation in focus. What can you see that's bothering you? What can you hear that's bothering you? Don't include guesses or interpretations, and try not to generalize. Don't make remarks such as "This is sabotage!" or "It's not always only about you, you know! Don't you care about my feelings?" Just describe what's happening: "We've agreed that you won't eat fattening foods in front of me. I can see you've got a sundae there." Later, you'll learn to expand on your feelings ("I'm feeling anxious, not to mention a bit jealous!") and make requests ("Please go somewhere else to eat that.").

Let's apply this idea to a more complex situation. Last night, Maria's mother fell at home and was in a lot of pain. Maria and her brother, Avery, took their mother straight to the hospital. The diagnosis was a broken hip, and their mother was admitted. One day later, Maria is aware of being angry at her brother. Maria's first task is to be clear with herself about which specific, objective behavior troubles her. She quickly identifies that. Avery has informed Maria that he made arrangements to have their mother admitted to a continuing care facility; when she's discharged from the hospital, she'll move right in. When Maria asked how he paid for it, her brother said, "Oh, I gave them her credit card number for a deposit." Clearly, Maria has a number of objective details to work with here.

You can see why it's always important to practice assertion only after making (at least mentally) a log entry and then asking the I AM WORTH IT questions. When the objective facts are clear-cut, Maria easily gets a yes to all of them.

Contrast this with a scenario in which Maria doesn't have a lot of objective data to work with. Let's say she's been telling her brother what she thinks is best for their mother now that she's broken her hip, but as she's talking, she thinks her brother has a snide smirk on his face. Even if she's convinced he's smirking at her, it is *not* grounds for action. Maybe his nose itches! Save your anger for what the person says or does, not what you think. If you base your request for change on thoughts rather than actions, you'll never get what you want. (What if Maria told her brother to wipe that smirk off his face, and he retorted, "You're seeing things! Where do you get off speaking to me that way?")

Armed with her four yes answers, Maria knows exactly what is upsetting her: Her brother is making decisions on his own about their mother's care. She also has the behavior she wants clearly in mind: She wants them to agree before either takes action, and she wants him to not consider his arrangements for the care facility as final until they've reached a joint decision.

When you do this yourself, remember: Don't waste your time with what you *don't* want; focus only on what you *do* want. Your objective is to rectify the situation. Avoid acting angrily, which will only decrease the likelihood that the other person will cooperate. Before you start, take a few slow, deep breaths to calm yourself. You want to say exactly what you mean. Keep it simple. Stick to what can be seen or heard.

Maria knows it's not in her best interest to accuse her brother of terrible behavior, because he would just get angry with her. Instead, she's going to concentrate exclusively on how she would like him to act. While he may not behave as she wants him to, she'll increase the chances that he will by 100 percent just by asking.

Maria says, "Avery, you just said that you've registered Mother at Fairway and given them her credit card number. You did this before we discussed options or agreed on a course of action." Now she can move on to the next step.

2. Report your feelings, if appropriate. Once she's stated the facts of the situation, Maria says, "I feel left out." Notice that she begins this sentence with an "I." Explaining your feelings about a situation by using "I" statements lets the other person know your motivation for changing their behavior, which tends to be more persuasive. People you care about generally don't want to see you troubled; in fact, all things being equal, many people will opt for the equilibrium of shared good feelings. (Bear in mind that if you're seeking change in a work situation, you need to be cautious about reporting your feelings in order to keep things professional. You may want to skip this step.)

Sometimes you may need to accommodate the other person's request as well. If it seems that's the case, your best bet is to begin including their thoughts and feelings from the beginning. Our colleague, Janet Macaluso, devised these questions to help open up the discussion.

- Do you have a different view?
- Do you feel different?
- What's your reaction to what I'm saying?

Before you make your request, it may be appropriate to give the other person a chance to speak. Listen with an open mind. Both of you will probably become more fully informed, and a mutually satisfactory course of action may be possible (a benefit for both of you) — or at least the distance between you may decrease.

3. **Request the specific behavior you want.** Asking for what you want may seem simple, but it's not easy to do. For one thing, you may have an entrenched habit of thinking "He should know what I want" or "She never does what I want—why should I even ask?" In taking the risk to make the request, you may not get what you ask for, and that refusal may force you to face up to bigger issues in your relationship. In some ways, letting your anger fester seems easier because as long as it stays inside, you *think* you're in control. Actually, the anger is controlling *you*.

By not requesting needed changes, you'll remain in a holding pattern of resentment that will block any positive development in the relationship. View assertion for what it is: a chance to get your needs met, yes, but also a chance to *improve* your relationship with the other person.

Let's consider a couple of examples. A co-worker returns from her break 15 minutes late, which isn't unusual for her. Lisa can't take a break until the other person returns.

- *Report the situation causing your negative thoughts and/or feelings:* "I was scheduled to go on break when you returned at 10:10. It's now 10:25."

- *Report your feelings, if appropriate:* Since it's a workplace situation, Lisa decides to skip this.

- *Request the specific behavior you want:* "Next time, please be back by 10:10." (In this situation, she may want to extract a promise, speaking in an even tone of voice and with neutral body language: "Is that something you can agree to do?")

In Maria's case, there's a lot at stake: their mother's future, her relationship with her brother, her sense of connection to her mother. She has stated the facts of the situation and told Avery how she feels. Now she has a two-part request for him.

- "In the future, when it comes to Mom's care, please wait until you and I have agreed on a plan before you take any action."

- "For now, please call the care facility and tell them to put the application on hold. Tell them that we'll be back in touch after you and I have had a chance to make a joint decision."

By articulating the situation and her feelings first, then making two very specific requests, Maria has greatly increased the chances that her request will be honored.

Reporting the situation and your feelings and then asking for a specific behavior are really the core of any request.

4. Acknowledge the difficulty the other person may have in complying. For most of us, the first three parts of a request are the toughest. Once you feel confident in the process of asserting yourself, you can start to add some flourishes that can increase your success and help to strengthen your relationships.

Just before you make your request, try acknowledging the difficulty the other person may have in complying. Comments such as "I know you had a busy day, too" not only show the other person that you care but also gain you tremendous negotiating power. Let's see how it works.

- *Report the situation causing your negative thoughts and/or feelings:* "When I walked into the kitchen this morning, the blender was still on the counter, and there were dirty dishes in the sink."

- *Report your feelings, if appropriate:* "I felt disappointed and annoyed."

- *Acknowledge the difficulty the other person may have in complying:* "I know it's quite late when you finish your snacks and that you're probably tired by then."

- *Request the specific behavior that you want:* "Still, I am asking you to clean up any mess before you go to bed."

That one extra sentence tells the person that you see his predicament, you feel for him, *and* you still need him to change his behavior. Try to avoid using the word *but* when you make your request, as it tends to give the impression that you're negating the other person's feelings in favor of your own needs.

5. Ask "Is that something you could do for me?" to extract a promise. You've moved all the way through the process, and you've clearly stated your request. If you suspect that you may meet resistance, or if it's a request that's been neglected in the past, you might follow up your request with an attempt to extract a promise. Then, if the situation reoccurs, or if your initial request was never honored, you can gently remind the other person of the previous promise.

6. State consequences only as a last resort. Occasionally, you may want to add an additional step—stating consequences—if you've followed the process outlined above, but it hasn't worked.

Consequences are a last resort. First, try several rounds of the first three steps. Keep in mind that your goal is not to annoy or put the other person down, but to get what you want. When in doubt, don't state consequences. You don't want to bluff or have your bluff called. Finally, *never threaten consequences that you don't want to have to implement.* This is especially important when dealing with a boss or a fragile situation.

Suppose Lisa's request that her co-worker return from her break on time hasn't succeeded, despite numerous conversations. It's time for her to add consequences: "The next time this week that you aren't back in time for my break, I'll have to ask our supervisor to establish another system for breaks." She hasn't set out to do this, because she knows it will cause tension in their relationship, but the co-worker has left her no other alternatives. If Lisa allows her co-worker to continue abusing the break schedule, she'll be swallowing her own thoughts and feelings, which would be completely unfair.

VIRGINIA LEARNS TO STAND UP FOR HERSELF

Of everything that has been helpful to me, developing the skill of assertion has been the most useful. Psychotherapy, Redford's cooperation, and sheer doggedness of effort have helped, too.

Gradually, I've learned to become more assertive. We belong to a marriage-enrichment group that meets every other week. About 15 years ago, at a time when I was trying hard to become more aware of negative feelings, I reported to the group that I had thrown a potholder across the kitchen at Redford when he had once again told me how to cook something I had already been preparing for an hour. The other couples in the group were astounded: prissy, proper, usually sweet Virginia letting it all hang out like that! Such an expression was a temporary stage for me — I needed to learn to articulate a better response than flinging a potholder! But at the time, even this kind of outburst represented progress over my more usual pattern of not realizing until later that Redford had annoyed me.

I've advanced to usually issuing more effective requests for changes in behavior. Sometimes it takes more than one round. Because practicing assertive behavior has traditionally been tough for me, I continually work on matters of modest size to keep me in practice — with no pouting or sulking allowed! Here's my current list.

- *All dinners include vegetables, regardless of who cooks.*
- *All work-related papers and other materials are kept in the study, not the living room, as agreed upon.*
- *Mail is removed from the kitchen counter the day it arrives, as agreed upon.*
- *When driving, don't exceed the speed limit by more than 5 mph if I'm in the car (never faster would be even better!).*
- *Everyone cleans up empty bottles, container caps, and other such messes.*
- *Not being interrupted.*
- *Getting equal airtime.*

By honing my assertion skill in these day-to-day matters, I've become more confident when tackling bigger issues. I've come a long way in confronting these larger concerns head-on.

- *Countering Redford's criticism by requesting that it stop*
- *Deciding when and how to take personal time for family and rest*
- *Dividing the work connected with having a family and running a household*

Now, when the thoughts and feelings that surround these more serious concerns begin to turn negative, I usually know how to handle them. Often, these bigger issues require mutual speaking, listening, and empathy. Redford and I have learned to ask each other, "Do you see this differently?" or "What's going on for you?"

Now it's your turn for some airtime. What's on your list?

LEARN TO SAY "NO"

You now have guidelines for asking for what you want. When dealing with another person, that suffices most of the time—but not always. Sometimes, negative feelings originate when others request something from you. Sometimes you may want to provide what is asked for, but other times you may prefer to say no. You need to be able to make that stick, without offending. The goal is to stay in control of how you invest your time, money, and good name.

Rachael Panther's straight black hair, round face, and dark olive skin, inherited from her Cherokee ancestors, were what you noticed first from a distance. Up close, her blue eyes—the legacy from her European forebears—were unexpected.

Rachael's social heritages were even more mixed. The Cherokee way considers the group first. Tribal councils are rather democratic, as they were long ago. In day-to-day activities, the pace of life accommodates the needs of those who require extra help or time. Early on, Rachael learned acceptance, patience, and consideration of the group's needs first.

From college professors and the media, she received different messages: to recognize personal needs and be true to herself. She was salutatorian of her class in high school, and in college, she quickly picked up both the intellectual content of her courses and a scrutinizing attitude that was new to her. With both her Cherokee heritage and her college insights vying for supremacy, sometimes Rachael wasn't clear about how she should behave.

Another part of her pre-college experience involved the role of women. In her community, most women strove to keep the family afloat, sometimes in the face of hardship. Mother's Day in the town of Cherokee, North Carolina, is celebrated with great fanfare in some families, including Rachael's. The celebrants often have much to be grateful for, and Rachael is among those who feel they owe their mothers a lot.

An important part of Rachael's family life was the church in which she grew up. The entire family sat in their usual pew each Sunday and attended all the revivals and potluck meals. Her preacher, who was deeply respected by most of his congregation, insisted that he thought of men and women as very different from each other. He placed a lot of emphasis on his interpretation of the words of the apostle Paul. From the preacher's perspective, Paul made it clear that women should subjugate individual desires whenever they were in conflict with biblical guidelines.

The Cherokee nation with which Rachael identified had suffered repeated assaults on their people and culture. In 1492, the Native American population was estimated at 5 million; four centuries later, it was 250,000, just 5 percent of its original size. The eastern band of Cherokees was estranged from those farther south who had earlier endured the deadly forced march westward to Oklahoma. Parents felt distant from their children, many of whom were shipped off to English-speaking boarding schools. This multigenerational trauma may help explain why Rachael's father, who had an alcohol problem, deserted the family when she was 3.

To Rachael, family was important. She was devoted to her mother, brother, sister, husband, and 2-year-old daughter. This devotion often translated into personal sacrifice; she rarely said no to anything that was asked of her. While she was putting herself through college, her unemployed brother once drove over to see Rachael in Asheville to ask for a loan. The following weekend, she worked an extra shift waiting tables, giving up study time to make up the rent money she'd given him.

As a grammar school teacher, Rachael showed this same commitment to her students. Those who came in early or stayed late could get any extra help they asked for. Even when it wasn't convenient for her to get to school early or stay late, Rachael almost always accommodated the students rather than asking them to come in at a time that better suited her.

Rachael was a sunny person. In any gathering, her voice rang out periodically with laughter. Her speech was idiosyncratic, with original phrases that grabbed your attention, all delivered in that soft western North Carolina drawl. Everyone liked Rachael a great deal, and they respected her — everyone, that is, except perhaps Rachael herself.

Rachael Needed to Keep Demands at a Reasonable Level

At many times in her life, dedication to the needs of others overwhelmed Rachael's own needs. A couple of years before we met her, she transferred to a larger school some distance away from her home to teach fourth grade. Soon after she arrived, she agreed to stay one evening for a special program for parents. Because it was poorly advertised, only one parent attended. When the administrator asked her to reschedule, she found herself saying yes, though she dreaded another evening away from her husband, Jerry, and their daughter, Suzy.

Rachael's principal quickly realized how agreeable she was. He frequently asked her to assume leadership for projects. Before long, she had twice as many extracurricular activities as most of the other teachers.

Rachael's family situation was similar. Would she lend her sister her car for the weekend? Could she babysit for her brother's child the same weekend? "Yes," she kept saying. At home, her husband saw her as solely responsible for housework and childcare.

But what about Rachael? She was exhausted most evenings. While she loved to go jogging along the beautiful woodland trails near her home, she rarely found the time. Even most of her weekends were spent doing things for others. When requests were made of her, Rachael needed to learn to say no —if not always, at least sometimes.

STAY IN BALANCE

Respecting the needs of both yourself and others is a tricky business. There's a middle ground that's best for everyone: keeping your close, supportive contact with others while reducing the demands on you to a more manageable level.

Recent studies of the stress response have found that women in particular rely heavily on social support to get them through tough times. Shelley Taylor, PhD, of UCLA found that women have a natural propensity to "tend and befriend" in times of severe stress—they honor their protective instincts over their families and other loved ones, and they seek out powerful alliances with those they believe can help them.[5]

Studies assembled by Barbara R. Sarason, PhD, a sociologist and emeritus professor at the University of Washington, and her colleagues suggest that social contact is usually beneficial to health, but not if it results in burdens that outweigh the benefits.[6] Rachael's situation was mixed: People were providing her with healthful social support, but she was failing to set limits that would protect her from taking on too much work.

To be truly in control, you need to learn how to avoid the twin pitfalls of isolation and overcommitment. If you find yourself continually reluctant to say no, it could be either a reflection of your innate personality or the result of modeling after a parent. Cultural standards, interpreted correctly or otherwise, may also be a factor.

Rachael needed to continue to acknowledge and respect the Cherokee way of concern for others, but she also had to ensure that it was a two-way street. When it wasn't, she needed to show herself the same consideration that she was showing others.

Let's take a look at three men: Jurgen, Tony, and Russ. They have similar jobs at a firm that designs graphics for information technology clients, but that's where the similarity ends. While Russ is enjoying a good life, Jurgen and Tony are stuck in counterproductive habits.

Jurgen tends to be a bit shortsighted when it comes to cooperation. Even when he has time to spare, he neglects to help his co-workers by giving their projects priority. When a colleague has a tight deadline, Jurgen very rarely pitches in to help with the work. Consequently, when he needs help with a heavy workload, no one offers.

Although his wife also has a job, Jurgen believes that all household chores—grocery shopping, planning meals, cooking, cleaning up, laundry, and housecleaning—are his wife's responsibility. She is usually tired and grouchy—and not coincidentally, their sex life is sporadic and unsatisfying. She spends most of her free time with girlfriends and her mother. When he's honest with himself, he admits that he's afraid the marriage may not last.

Jurgen never helps out any community groups, such as a church, the Red Cross, the Little League, or his town's soup kitchen. He'll tell anyone who will listen how these kinds of institutions are insincere, encourage bad habits, or are riddled with corruption. He has plenty of free time—the problem is that no one wants to spend it with him! He himself will admit that he wishes he had more buddies and a better relationship with his wife. He acknowledges that he doesn't seem to get as much satisfaction out of his life as most people do. He vaguely recognizes the complete lack of warm human contact in his life, but he remains oblivious to the reasons that other people avoid him.

On the flip side, there's Tony. He's always helping co-workers by letting them speak first, giving their projects priority, and pitching in to help with deadlines. When there's a job for two, his colleagues fight to be his partner.

Tony can be counted on to come in early, stay late, be responsible for the first draft, and pitch in on all revisions.

At home, too, he does the bulk of the chores: He buys groceries on the way home, fixes dinner most nights, and helps with the cleanup. He's good at laundry and cleaning, too. Although he has two siblings, it's Tony who always takes their mother to doctors' appointments.

A number of community groups depend on Tony as well. At his church, he's head of the annual canvass to solicit financial pledges as well as chairman of the annual auction. And he's a Cub Scout leader. When everyone else has said no, Tony has always been there, so people now come to him *first*. As a result, many of his associates are developing the bad habit of not pulling their fair share of the load. Tony is busy for more than 100 hours a week. He has no time to himself. He feels tired, anxious, a little depressed, and sometimes overwhelmed.

And then there's Russ. While he sometimes helps out his colleagues, he has no trouble saying "Not this time" when he has too much to do. He and his wife, who also works, split chores fairly evenly, regularly rotating their least and most favorite tasks—and making sure they take a second to laugh during their negotiations. When relatives need a hand, they may hear a yes or a no, depending on Russ's schedule and energy level. He limits himself to situations he considers important, and he balances his own needs with those of others. He belongs to a synagogue and one community service group, but he sets a limit on the number of hours he devotes per month.

By being conscious of where he spends his time and taking a moment to consider before he commits, Russ enjoys close ties to his wife, his family, and his community. He has time for himself, too.

Are you more like Jurgen, Tony, or Russ?

Finding the right mix between respecting your own needs and the needs of others may take some trial and error; this balancing act may be hard to master. Your first task is figuring out if you really *want* to say no; then you have to learn to make that answer stick.

KNOW HOW YOU WANT TO SPEND YOUR TIME

Before you can learn the art of saying no, you need to clarify your own priorities. Only then can you use your energy thoughtfully and deliberately.

Let's give some thought to how you want to portion out your time, money, and good name. You may need to weigh tradeoffs, but whatever you decide, try to limit your total commitments in all areas to a reasonable load. Otherwise, you're likely to perform badly everywhere, have insufficient funds to purchase what you most need, and find your reputation compromised.

How much time do you plan to devote to work? For many of us, juggling how we invest life's greatest resource — our time — begins with deciding how much of it to devote to work.

Statistics abound suggesting that, as a society, Americans often give preference to work over other options. Workers in the United States recently surpassed the diligent Japanese in the number of hours on the job. The Bureau of Labor Statistics reported in 2001 that more than 25 million Americans worked at least 49 hours a week in 1999. Eleven million of those said they worked more than 59 hours a week.[7]

As technology has come to play an increasing role in most jobs, the game of balancing work versus nonwork time now occurs on a new playing field. Laptop computers, mobile phones, personal digital assistants, and wireless and high-speed Internet access have increased efficiency, freeing an increasing number of workers from the constraints of location by allowing distance connections or telecommuting. The downside is that the line between when you're working and when you're not has, in many cases, blurred to the point of nonexistence.

The balance between future career rewards and present quality of life comes into play, too. Working long hours is one strategy for advancing professionally, yet if you take this route, what time and energy are left for your personal life? Trying to have both a successful professional life *and* a fulfilling personal life may involve a precarious balancing act. When both partners in a couple work outside the home, the housework and other chores still have to be done. Add children to the picture, and the situation becomes even more difficult. The time crunch is even greater for single parents.

In your notebook, prioritize your list of values. Do you want to:

- Enjoy close family ties?

- Raise well-adjusted children?

- Be able to afford a good education for your children?

- Be financially secure by age 50?

- Be listed in *Who's Who?*

- Improve the well-being of those less fortunate than yourself?

- Improve the well-being of the planet?

- Protect your health through exercise?

- Impress everyone at your high school reunion by how good you look after all that exercise?

- Impress everyone at your high school reunion with your achievements?

Living in accord with your list is challenging but can be quite satisfying. With that list of values/priorities in hand, get out your calendar and look at your appointments for the last month or two. Being honest with yourself, can you say there's congruence between your list and how you're spending your time?

How do you want to spend your money? For most of us, finances are a limited resource; even if you have plenty of money, you don't have an *infinite* supply. In order to help your money give you the kind of life you want, you have to think about it and allot it carefully, not just react to demands and whims. What are your financial priorities? Do you want to:

- Enjoy good times while you're still young?

- Feel secure in your old age?

- Provide funds for your children's education?

- Share a portion of your wealth with the less fortunate?

- Support nonprofit groups?

- Help relatives?

- Collect a great wardrobe?

- Create a place you like calling home?

- Drive a new car?

- Have a gourmet kitchen?

- Have an adequate emergency fund for unexpected situations?

- Take dream vacations?

We know that old-fashioned budgeting is no fun. But if you begin to view your finances as an opportunity to live and honor your own priorities, you'll find it a lot easier to spend less in some areas so you can spend more in others.

To what do you want to lend your good name? Often, we are asked to lend our endorsement to others, whether it be someone who needs a job reference, a salesperson who'd like you to present her project to your company, or even a candidate asking you to campaign on his behalf. If you receive requests to endorse groups, ask yourself if you agree with their message; imagine that your audience will substitute your name for theirs. In each case, are you willing to endorse:

- An established community group?

- A new community group?

- A community cause?

- A new club?

- Someone's moneymaking scheme?

- A new business?

- A political action committee?

We sometimes recommend people or things because it's easier than saying no, but what are the long-term effects? Try to remain aware of all the consequences of each particular bid for your support.

HAVE A SYSTEM FOR RESPONDING TO REQUESTS

Once you've completed the difficult business of deciding what you want most, you need to plan ahead so you don't get sidetracked from your goals. We recommend the following method.

Delay your response, if necessary. When someone asks you for your time or money or to lend your name to something, take as much time as you need to really think about how you want to answer. You may need a few seconds, a few minutes, a few days, or, rarely, a month or more. Make this your mantra: "Let me think about that and get back to you (in an hour, tomorrow, next week)." The other person will see that you're carefully weighing the request, and you'll have a chance to figure out what you really want. If someone pressures you by insisting on a decision right away, simply say, "Well, then, I'm going to have to say no."

Tune in to your thoughts and feelings. Once you've bought yourself some time, write down the request, look at it for a minute, then turn your thoughts inside: What do you think about what's being asked of you? Maybe you think, "Wow, that will be really interesting!" or "What a career opportunity!"

On the other hand, you may find yourself thinking, "When will I ever find time?" or "Surely I'm not the only one who could do this!"

Perhaps your thoughts are some combination of interest and trepidation. Write down all of your reactions. Are you pleased? Upset? Disgusted?

Sad? Feeling trapped? Just observe and record for now. You're collecting data that will help you make your decision.

Ask questions to decide whether to say yes or no. If you experience a mixture of positive and negative, you'll have to be particularly careful as you think through what you want your decision to be. Ask the I AM WORTH IT questions.

1. Is saying yes or no Important to me? This is straightforward.

2. Is what I am thinking or feeling Appropriate to what is being asked of me? Your positive and negative feelings need to be sorted out to see if one side predominates. If not, the last two questions may help you decide on your response.

3. Is the situation Modifiable? Can I say no?

4. When I balance the needs of myself and others, is saying no **WORTH IT**? If the situation involves a family member, you may need to weigh your answer carefully; if the request comes from your boss, the answer could well be "No, it's not worth it."

Remember, answering yes to the questions means you will say no to the request.

Now you're ready for the big moment. It's time to say no—and feel good about doing it!

Keep your "no" short and explicit—and don't justify it. Learn to embrace the simple beauty of the answer "no." Complete in and of itself, it needs no further explanation. If you choose to give one, keep it short, especially when dealing with someone who's likely to argue.

If this seems harsh, you can soften your refusal by acknowledging the perspective of the person making the request.

- "I know it's important to you to find a coach. But sorry, I need to say no."

- "I know you're working on a really important project, but I need to say no."

- "I know finding a chair of that committee is important, but I need to say no."

You *never* want to offer a long explanation about why you need to say no. If you give one, you may find that you end up talking not about your refusal but about the adequacy of your explanation. If you aren't careful, the discussion will shift to how little of your time, money, or inconvenience would be involved!

Watch Susan take on a commitment she wanted to avoid, and notice how she allows herself to be roped in.

Elliott: "Susan, you know I've coached the soccer team for a year now."

Susan: "Yes, and you've done a great job."

Elliott: "Thanks. It's been good to have your help on occasion."

Susan: "I was glad to give it."

Elliott: "It's good to have these positions rotated."

Susan: "It certainly is!"

Elliott: "I'm glad you agree, because the team needs you to coach them next year."

Susan: "Surely there must be someone else!"

Elliott: "There is no one else."

Susan: "Have you checked with Jamil or Clara?"

Elliott: "Would you do that? And I'll assume that we can count on you if they say no."

Susan: "But I'm too busy already. I really don't have the time, especially with the baby and everything."

Elliott: "It won't take that much time. You're going to be surprised how little it takes."

Susan: "But the baby . . ."

> *Elliott:* "Don't worry about the baby. We'll have some of the players on the bench take turns babysitting. I'm so glad we can count on you, Susan. Thanks."

In her effort to be polite, Susan has given Elliott the means to weaken her own argument. In contrast, watch Gary, whom Elliott had asked first, say no effectively. Gary already has what he considers a full load of family, community, and professional responsibilities.

> *Elliott:* "Gary, you know I've coached the soccer team for a year now."
>
> *Gary:* "Yes, and you've done a great job."
>
> *Elliott:* "Thanks. It's been good to have your help on occasion."
>
> *Gary:* "I was glad to give it."
>
> *Elliott:* "It's good to have these positions rotated. I see you aren't coaching softball next year."
>
> *Gary:* "That's right, I'm not."
>
> *Elliott:* "The soccer team needs you to coach them."
>
> *Gary (after pausing for several seconds):* "I hear you saying that the team needs me to coach them next year, but I must say no."
>
> *Elliott:* "There may be no one else."
>
> *Gary:* "I still need to say no."
>
> *Elliott:* "It wouldn't take much time."
>
> *Gary:* "I still need to say no."
>
> *Elliott:* "Why can't you?"
>
> *Gary:* "I just know that I need to say no to any new responsibilities. Sorry."

Avoid being drawn into apology or debate when saying no. Susan got trapped because she reflexively offered a reason. She also may not have been absolutely sure she felt good about saying no.

In contrast, when Gary was first asked, he took a few seconds to pay

---

How to Say No

1. Delay your response, if necessary.
2. Keep it simple.
3. Always include an explicit "No."
4. Don't justify.

---

attention to his thoughts and feelings. He realized he had negative thoughts and probably negative feelings about taking on an additional burden, so he asked the I AM WORTH IT questions. Sure, the matter was important, his thoughts and feelings were appropriate, and it was possible that he could say no. When he considered the balance of his own needs and prior commitments and those of the team and the present coach, he knew it would be worth it to decline the request. Having done his homework, he was armed with his four yes answers and could be confident that he could say no explicitly. Knowing that he had justified the decision to himself *before* he gave Elliott an answer, Gary was at ease; he didn't need to justify it to Elliott. He knew it was he, not Elliott, who should be in control here.

Regularly Seek Relief

Don't just sit around waiting for opportunities to show off your assertiveness skill by saying no. In fact, it's good to have that little bit of cushion in your life so that if the right opportunity comes along, you can welcome it with an enthusiastic "Yes!"

Make it a habit to regularly look at where you are now and where you'd like to go in the future. Constantly ask yourself, "Do I really want to be doing this?"

Peer into the future. Are situations likely to come up where you will be asked for your time, money, or good name? Open your notebook and list them, then quickly ask yourself the I AM WORTH IT questions for each

(continued on page 160)

Field Guide

THE PTA

When your son enters high school, you follow your previous pattern of joining the PTA and become treasurer. In the ensuing months, you have reason to regret your actions.

This group devotes most of its time to fund-raising rather than hands-on projects and open forums. Funds raised from the projects this year are to be used for extra equipment for the library and uniforms for the new band members.

You don't object to these projects, but keeping the books straight is proving to be a challenge, especially because the money tends to trickle in person by person.

Even worse, the principal has informed you that ordering the equipment and band uniforms falls within the responsibilities of the PTA treasurer. You had assumed you would hand over the money to school personnel who would be responsible for making the purchases.

You're immediately aware of feelings of distaste at the prospect of having to hassle with outside companies. You feel annoyed and put-upon, so you ask the four I AM WORTH IT questions.

1. Yes, it is **I**mportant to you that you are being asked to assume this task.
2. Yes, it is **A**ppropriate to be annoyed that school personnel are trying to fob off their work onto you.
3. Yes, you could **M**odify this situation by refusing to assume this responsibility.

4. Yes, taking action would be **WORTH IT.**

You call the principal to set up a meeting and tell the person who answers the phone that you want to talk about the role of the treasurer in regard to upcoming orders. The morning of the meeting, after an exchange of pleasantries, you tell the principal that when you accepted the position of treasurer, no one mentioned that the responsibilities included ordering uniforms and audiovisual equipment. This is not a responsibility you are willing to assume.

The principal explains that previous treasurers had done the ordering.

You reply, "I hear you saying that previous treasurers did the ordering. I understand that you would rather not have your staff do this extra work, but this is not a responsibility I am willing to assume."

"But other treasurers have done the ordering."

"Other treasurers may have done the ordering, but it's not a responsibility I am willing to assume. If that's necessary to this office, I will need to resign."

"No, no, that won't be necessary. We'll take care of ordering the uniforms and audiovisual equipment," the principal says. After a pause, he adds, "There's another matter I would like us to discuss. We're going to need a capable parent for another project coming up next year."

You smile. "I'd love to hear about that. When we do talk about it, it would be helpful if I could have a list of all the responsibilities so I can think about what would be involved before I decide if I'm interested."

one. Next, select only those situations where you have gotten four yes answers. These are the ones in which you will need to say no. Circle them or write them in a separate list.

Now, think through your plan to keep your answer clear and definite. Next to each situation, write down your strategy for how you will say no.

Ask for help or relief when you can't say no. Even if saying no at work isn't an option, you still have a number of ways to stay in at least partial control when you are feeling overwhelmed. If you want to work less or just continue to perform well at existing tasks, try these approaches with your supervisor or whoever else has authority over you.

- **Discuss your current duties and responsibilities with your boss and ask for input on prioritizing the new request, taking other responsibilities into account:** "Before I was asked to create the new manual, I'd been working about 48 hours a week to stay on top of the Smith and Hammonds projects and get out that big mailing. What priority would you like me to give the manual relative to the other tasks?"

- **Discuss whether there is anything on your list that can be discarded or delegated:** "Here are the hours I've been working for the past 2 weeks to stay on top of the Smith project, the Hammonds project, and the mailing to small businesses in the fourth district, with the relative number of hours spent on each. I don't think it's possible to add the creation of a new manual and keep my current responsibilities afloat. Can any of this be discarded or delegated to someone else?"

- **Clarify timelines for the items on your list:** "Here are my current responsibilities: the Smith project, the Hammonds project, the mailing to small businesses in the fourth district, and the new manual. Would you clarify for me what you see as the standards by which each will be evaluated and when you expect each to be completed?"

These suggestions may or may not succeed in reducing the demands placed on you, but at the very least, you've drawn attention to your plight and put the responsibility on your supervisor's shoulders. You've warned him that you're already surpassing the traditional workweek hours by 20 percent per week, and you're concerned that if you're given this new responsibility, you won't be able to devote adequate attention to all the projects. (If you still receive no relief, consider documenting this conversation in case one of your projects falls short of expectations and others attempt to hold you responsible. At least you'll have proof that you attempted to rectify the situation.)

Can you think of any situations that you need to address with authority figures in which you probably shouldn't say no, but you need guidance or help to prioritize? Which of the three possible approaches do you plan to use?

Jettison some current responsibilities. Dumping responsibilities you already have can be difficult—albeit a heavenly idea! All of us have things we don't want to do, but some of them are necessary. How do you tell the difference?

Again, start by listening to your feelings and thoughts about a specific task. If they're negative, ask the I AM WORTH IT questions. If you get four yes answers, it's time to act.

First, formulate action steps and a timetable for ridding yourself of the responsibility. Ask yourself, "To whom do I need to speak?" and "By what date will I complete this?" If the date arrives and you still have the responsibility, use problem-solving to figure out what else you need to do, then revise the timetable.

RACHAEL LEARNS TO BALANCE HER NEEDS WITH OTHERS'

Learning to say no effectively wasn't easy for Rachael. In our workshop, she quickly realized that she said yes much too often. She revisited incident after incident and recognized what an entrenched pattern this had become in her life. She could also see it was going to be a challenge to break those habits.

"Let's assume that your sister has once again asked to borrow your car for the weekend," we said. "What are you likely to feel if she makes that request?"

"I'm not sure," Rachael answered. "She's my sister."

We asked her to locate her feelings on the continuum that shows positive feelings on the right and negative feelings on the left. Rachael placed a mark way to the left. Eventually, she specified feelings of concern.

When she answered the I AM WORTH IT questions, she soon had four yes answers. Her car was important to her, and her negative feelings about her sister's request . . . well, perhaps they were appropriate. (Rachael was quite tentative on this second question.) Gradually, it began to dawn on her that she could indeed say no. She allowed herself the luxury of imagining it, and in her mind's eye, she could see that her family—she, Jerry, and Suzy—would be better off. Soon, she warmed to the idea that if she learned to stand on her own two feet, even her sister would be better off.

Then Rachael practiced her response. She got another workshop participant to play the persistent persuader. At first, she made the mistake of offering explanations, which could immediately become the point of focus: "Sis, I can't lend you my car for the weekend. I've already agreed to pick up some school supplies."

The person role-playing her sister had a quick retort: "Oh, I can work around that. I'll just borrow your car next weekend!"

Rachael was caught. She went back to the I AM WORTH IT questions and remembered her yes answers. She also remembered that when she thought about her sister's request, one of her feelings was concern. Besides, Rachael liked having her car available every weekend! She had put a lot of resources into purchasing it, and now she was being asked to give it up. It should be her decision. She needed to say no and leave it at that.

After a few rounds of being sabotaged by her explanations, Rachael learned to keep her answer simple. Still, as a warm person, she found it best to acknowledge the other person's perspective first.

Finally, she was able to say, "I understand you would like to be able to go to Asheville this weekend and then have my car for side trips. I still need to say no."

After this initial example, Rachael practiced again and again. She used other situations, such as the requests from her principal, which were directed at her more often than at the other teachers. Finally, she felt ready to think about the distribution of work at home.

"Jerry comes home and relaxes. I pick up Suzy, drive home, start supper, fix Suzy a snack, and put a load of laundry in the washer," Rachael explained.

"And how do you feel about that?" we asked.

"Tired."

"Tired" didn't sound like a very good place to be. Rachael eventually realized that taking on all the family's responsibilities was probably harming them as much as it was tiring her out. When she thought about it, she was sure the whole family would benefit if she said no once in a while. How would Suzy ever learn to be an independent, accountable person if she wasn't given any chores appropriate to her age? How would she view the role of women if Jerry didn't pitch in as well?

Once Rachael started saying no more often, her relatives began to depend on themselves more. Happily, they still seemed to love her at least as much as before. And, as a bonus, their pride in their own abilities increased.

At school, Rachael learned how to say no to her principal and—miraculously!—the distribution of work become more equitable. "Sorry," Rachael would say, "I'm only scheduling one extra evening for parents who missed the usual conference time." She could direct May Day or organize the schoolwide museum trip, but not both; someone else would need to take the other responsibility. She was also working toward extricating herself from responsibilities she had already agreed to take on. Rachael was no longer a pushover.

By being self-protective, Rachael came into her own. As she became more balanced in her own life, she was even more respected by her family, her students, and her colleagues. Now, Rachael was on her way to being one of life's big winners. Go, Rachael!

Week 5 Recap

Assertion

1. When you're aware of negative thoughts and feelings, ask the I AM WORTH IT questions.

2. If you get four yeses, determine if it's the behavior of another person that's causing you distress.

3. If it is, you need to ask the person in very specific terms to change. You can do this by:

- Reporting the situation: State in a couple of sentences what's causing you distress; keep it brief, stick to facts, and don't attack the other person
- If appropriate, describing your feelings regarding the situation at hand, using "I" statements
- Requesting the specific behavior that you want

You can also consider:

- Showing empathy for the other person's point of view
- Extracting a promise
- Stating consequences (but only as a last resort)

Saying No

1. Decide on your priorities in terms of how you want to portion out your time, money, and good name.

2. Pay attention to your thoughts and feelings whenever something is asked of you. Delay your response until you have figured them out. If they're negative, ask:

- Is it Important to me that I am being asked to invest my time, energy, money, or good name in this undertaking?
- Are my thoughts and feelings about this request Appropriate?
- Can I Modify this situation? (Under most circumstances, you can say no to whatever is being asked of you, so the answer here is usually yes.)
- When I consider my needs and those of others, is saying no WORTH IT?

3. Four yes answers means you need to say no to the requests.

4. To make your answer stick, keep your no short and explicit and don't justify it.

CHAPTER 8

WEEK 6: IMPROVE COMMUNICATION WHEN SPEAKING AND LISTENING

No one is listened to—*really* listened to—all the time. This week, however, you'll find out how to speak in ways that help others stay open to what you have to say. You'll also learn the reverse: how to listen effectively, using quiet and appropriate body language that signals you're paying close attention. In addition, you'll become proficient at balancing the amount of time you speak and listen.

For almost 18 years, Margaret Polascik had worked for the department of education in a state capital. She always took care to be professionally dressed when at work. Her curly brown hair was cut short, and her skin was still fairly smooth and youthful for a woman in her late forties.

Although her facial expression was always attentive, Margaret tended to say little unless she was pressed. When she did speak, even on subjects she passionately cared about, her face and body remained quite still.

Margaret's life revolved around her job. Divorced, she lived alone; her grown son was successfully independent and living in another city. Margaret tended to get to work early and stay late, and sometimes she even went in on weekends. Indeed, most of Margaret's life energy was directed toward her passion for developing and implementing improvements in education.

Exceptionally knowledgeable and devoted to her job, Margaret should have stood out among officials connected with the department. She was the most savvy and dedicated member of a group of committed professionals, which was no small feat. She had as much education as the others, and she attended several national conferences each year, even footing the bill for some of them so she could stay up-to-date on current developments.

Margaret was full of good ideas for improving education in her state. Her knowledge of the dynamics of school improvement, the workings of the education committees in the legislature, and the perspectives of the many state school districts was more complete than that of anyone else at her level. She was on a mission. Yet for all of her great ideas and passionate commitment, she rarely proposed major initiatives. When her opinion was sought, she tended to speak in the most general terms. Others would put forth the specifics, and when it was time to appoint committees to investigate promising avenues of change, they were selected to serve, not Margaret. Even when she was appointed to committees, she would do the work and someone else would get the credit.

Nevertheless, Margaret slowly made her way up the career ladder. At every stage, she functioned as if she were responsible for everything that happened within the department. On several occasions, Margaret's supervisor at the time either resigned or was transferred, and each time, she was made acting head, with explicit instructions to maintain the status quo. Without fail, officials would appoint someone else to the permanent position. It was only when that person left, usually soon afterward, that Margaret was appointed permanently.

Each time she was tapped for the next position up, her responsibilities had already been narrowed due to the incompetence or limitations of the short-term supervisor who preceded her. By the time we met her, Margaret had been in her current position for several years, and she seemed to be permanently stuck just below the level that would let her be a key decision maker.

Having no voice in departmental decision making was hurting not only Margaret but also the policies coming out of the department. If she had possessed more authority, the policies would have been more nuanced, with many parties' interests represented and balanced. She had big plans to juggle the needs of rural *communities, the inner suburbs, the outer suburbs, and the cities themselves. She was especially keen to set aside money for early childhood education, better-quality reading programs, and opportunities for teachers to continue learning. Because she had managed to balance all of these plans within the proposed budgets, she'd cleverly devised a way to give attention to the needs of each geographic and economic constituency, which would nearly ensure passage of her proposal in the two houses of the state legislature.*

Instead, these ideas and others—such as Internet connections, background checks for school bus drivers, and help with advanced-placement courses—were lying dormant in Margaret's head, just like her own potential for greatness.

Margaret Needed to Speak So Others Would Pay Attention

Margaret's promotion was clearly in her own self-interest as well as in the interest of her organization and the citizens of her state. So why hadn't it happened?

While there's no single answer, part of the explanation lies in her lack of speaking skill. Before expressing her opinion, Margaret waited to be asked. She might be sitting at the table with a huge concern, but if no one else brought it up, it didn't get on the collective agenda.

There was another factor that made it a challenge for Margaret to be noticed: She was too good at delegating. While delegating often works well, Margaret was applying it when she should not have. In an attempt to shield herself while forwarding her own ideas, she'd become very good at working through others. After developing an entire proposal, she'd hand it over to someone else within the department and allow that person to present it as his own. Margaret provided the labor; someone else collected the credit.

Why Margaret had come to be so self-effacing isn't easily answered. Perhaps she was one of those naturally shy individuals we discussed in the first chapter. Perhaps she had modeled herself on a beloved relative. Perhaps when she began her career, she came up against gender expectations and fashioned her behavior accordingly.

Whatever the origins of her reticence and fear of speaking up, Margaret's behavior provided at least part of the explanation for the slow pace at which she had risen within the department. The word I was almost totally absent from her vocabulary. She needed to present her ideas as her own and do it more assertively, in order to get the credit she deserved. But perhaps the biggest thing that she needed to do was the one thing she was most afraid of: She had to retain leadership. Whenever there was a job opening that would be a promotion for her, Margaret waited to be asked or appointed instead of coming forward to suggest, with documentation, why she was the most qualified.

She also had a habit of withholding key information when she was presenting her conclusions. Of course, she had reams of information—she always did her research, and she had years of experience. Yet she often failed to articulate any details about why she had reached a particular conclusion or why a program would stand a better chance of being funded if presented in a particular way. As a result, her proposals foundered, as did she.

One key factor that Margaret also overlooked was body language. While she was attentive when others were speaking, her expression was flat and her body unanimated when she was doing the talking. The way she presented her ideas never demonstrated to her supervisors how excited and passionate she was about providing a quality education for every child in the state. This lack of energy made it more difficult for people to listen, which in turn doomed her proposals.

While Margaret may not have been born to be a public speaker, she could succeed by following the speaking guidelines to convey her enthusiasm and deep knowledge. This would help her to connect with her listeners and get her excellent ideas heard.

As we've said, it's never too late. Margaret already had many positive traits— she was passionate, optimistic, and good at problem solving—but now she needed to learn to speak up in ways that would be heard.

GET HEARD

Congratulations! With Week 6, you move from dealing with the "bad stuff"—finding ways to get over your negative feelings and thoughts and resolving bad situations—and get into the "good stuff." From this point, you will learn to communicate more effectively, focus on the positive, and get what you most want out of life.

The ability to express our ideas well increases our ability to influence our fate. Falling short here can hamper us in many ways. Margaret's problems occurred at work. For others, the challenge may be on the home front. Wherever we find ourselves, learning to speak effectively is the only way to get our own agendas moving. Let's look at several individuals who are not yet great speakers, beginning with Henry.

Henry has worked for several different companies. Each time, he has moved up to midlevel responsibility, and there his progress halted. When downsizing came, Henry always found himself among those who were let go. When a company needs to cut somewhere, supervisors reason that it makes sense to keep those who have stood out as clearly indispensable. Even though he's hardworking and has performed well in every task assigned to him, you'll never hear Henry blabbing about that. Consequently, nobody knows.

In his present job, Henry devised a plan to restructure an operation in his division. He worked out all the details and did a cost analysis; the only thing left was to ask to present it at one of the regularly scheduled meetings. Instead, he showed it to several colleagues. One suggested a few changes and, in the process, quickly and quietly took over the project as his own. Of course, Henry's idea was a success, but when credit was passed out, it was the colleague who reaped the kudos.

Sally, on the other hand, likes to fill the air with "conversation," although she doesn't seem to notice that real conversation usually involves give and take. She regularly dominates most of the talk over the breakfast table, while her two kids struggle to get in a sentence or two. Her husband, Frank, has given up; from behind his newspaper or his thin smile, he mentally shuts them all out.

Before pulling up to Sally's house, whoever is driving the carpool that day switches to the all-news station on the radio—better nonstop news than nonstop chatter. At meetings, others struggle to get a word in edgewise when Sally pauses to catch her breath; sometimes she even talks over them once she sees an opening. People are even starting to avoid her in the cafeteria. Sally needs to learn to take turns.

Unlike Sally, Bill *never* speaks up at home. During dinner, he'll answer questions if asked, but he never chatters on voluntarily. Acquaintances avoid him at parties and during the break in his evening class. Sitting with Bill at lunch must be boring, too, because people always pass him over when looking for a place to sit. As an eating partner who never initiates a discussion and replies to questions with one-word answers, Bill's not what you would call a lively conversationalist. His co-workers have concluded that they have better ways to spend their free time than trying to drag a few words out of him.

But Bill may have bigger problems: He's now worried that his wife, Fay, may be having an affair. She used to talk to him all the time, pleading with him to tell her what he was feeling and thinking. Now she rarely asks. Like Sally, Bill needs to learn to take turns, but for him, the first hurdle is simply to start talking.

Each of these people is having trouble getting their own good ideas and friendly personalities across, either by not speaking up enough to let people in on their thoughts or by speaking up so much that no one cares to listen anymore. Human beings are social animals, and much of what we do and accomplish in the world is tied to how we present ourselves. You may have the best design or product or heart in the world, but no one will know it unless you open your mouth—effectively—and put your views into the best words and deeds possible.

Speak Up for the Right Amount of Time

Good communication is largely about timing. We've all had those moments when we're driving home from work and remember a conversation from earlier in the day. How often do you come up with the perfect answer or witty retort hours after the conversation has ended? You can't control these off-the-cuff conversations, much as you'd like to go back in time. What you can do is plan and prepare for those conversations you *do* know you'll be having and just hit them out of the park. Once you have a few successful presentations or discussions under your belt, you'll be a lot more confident and be able to speak in ways that will get you heard in other situations.

Preparation is everything—especially if you find speaking up to be a challenge. Try a few of these tips as you go forward.

Just do it. The first part of communicating is to just go ahead and speak! This is harder for some people than for others. If you are shy or reserved, you may have to make a particular effort to initiate a conversation. Push yourself a bit to start talking with another person. When a co-worker tells you about her family, report something about your own. When a friend describes why he liked a recent movie, explain why you liked or disliked that film or comment on another you've seen. If you haven't seen any movies, talk about a book you've read or a restaurant you've tried—anything about which you can give your opinion. Talk to bank tellers, store clerks, or the person in line in front of you at a sporting event. If the conversation doesn't go well, it will be over in seconds, and you can move on to the next one. The key here is practice: The more you do it, the easier it is.

At work, if you have your own chatterbox like Sally who has just finished a 10-minute treatise on her vacation, wait until she draws a breath, then say, "That sounds great. I was just on vacation, too. I went . . ." and take the opportunity to share your trip with her. The good thing about trying this out on someone like Sally is that you don't have to worry about boring her, since she's certainly done that to you often enough, and she's probably just waiting for her next opening to speak. Who knows? You may help teach her some patience.

Seek out those who listen. Another fail-safe tactic for the shy is to seek out the company of good listeners. This approach would work well for

Bill—he could use a bit of practice in getting out two or three consecutive sentences. Henry might use such a listener for dry runs on expressing his ideas all the way through, to decrease the likelihood that his kernel of a good idea will be developed by someone else.

Monitor your own airtime. If speaking or initiating a conversation is easy for you, be sure you share the floor. Give others a chance to speak. One way you could do this is to keep a rough tally on some occasions of how much you talk and how much others do. If it's you and one other person, is the airtime roughly 50/50? If it's a group of, say, six people, are you talking about a sixth of the time and listening the rest? In addition, you could ask a good friend how you split listening and speaking. While that perspective may be less reliable, depending on the source, it's still valuable. Sally could certainly benefit greatly from these exercises!

Forcing yourself to speak up for the right amount of time will probably seem awkward at first, but it's important to just get started. With practice, you'll feel much less self-conscious.

Make "I" Statements

As we mentioned earlier, "I" statements can be very helpful in contentious situations because they let you describe your feelings without directly accusing the other party of having caused them. They permit the listener to either agree or disagree with what you've said. Not using them can actually make others resent you.

For example, one day Sally strode into a meeting and pronounced, "This room is too cold!" Two people, already seated, exchanged glances. One rolled her eyes, and the other nodded knowingly. They probably would have reacted differently if Sally had come into the room, sat down, and then said, "I feel cold." Most people would be more likely to offer a sweater or turn up the thermostat.

In the first case, Sally was deciding for everyone in the room. In the second case, she was speaking only for herself and letting others know where she was coming from. While the temperature of a room is hardly something that can cause significant rifts in relationships, it does hint at the danger of blanket pronouncements. If Sally had been talking about a more controversial topic, such as child rearing, gender roles, or how to spend department funds, she probably would have turned some people off. By acknowledging that what she's saying comes from her own perspective, she may be able to soften this reaction.

These same "I" statements can help you share more of your personality with those around you and claim your own opinions. The more you use "I" statements when it comes to your own ideas, the more credit you'll be given for them. The rule is simple: Whenever possible, make "I" statements.

Report Your Feelings, if Appropriate

You may not be an expert about everything, but you are a world-class expert in what you're feeling: angry, sad, fearful, disgusted, joyful, interested, surprised, contemptuous, ashamed, or even loving. Or you may be experiencing some degree of one of these feelings. Anger, for example, can range from mild annoyance to rage. Reporting your feelings is the best way to let someone truly know what's happening with you. This simple act will help you connect with the other person, even if you're reporting negative feelings.

Particularly in your personal relationships, reporting your feelings is likely to get you heard. Since only you know how you feel, what you say is likely to be of great interest to the other person. If it's a negative feeling, she may be moved to help you get over it. If it's a good feeling, sharing that could lead her to share it with you, particularly if she's the reason for your joy. You may even be encouraging her to continue!

Let's say that instead of telling her husband, Frank, for the umpteenth time, "You aren't giving me enough attention!" Sally said, "I feel lonely." Frank could be a great rescuing hero rather than an insensitive clod centered only on himself.

Bill is disappointed that he and Fay can't join some of their friends on a weekend trip to the beach because they don't have the money. Even if Bill has learned to speak up, he needs to learn the most effective way to get his message across. "If you didn't spend all that money on clothes, we wouldn't be stuck here every holiday!" is much less likely to elicit Fay's interest in saving for such a trip than "I feel disappointed that we can't make that trip." Indeed, instead of attacking him about what a poor provider he is or how much money he wastes, Fay can be the rescuer who helps him get over the disappointment, as opposed to being cast as the spendthrift.

Temper your words at work. In a business situation, reporting feelings may not always be appropriate. In some cases, though, it can be—at least in a somewhat watered-down version.

The colleague who took Henry's idea never learned that Henry was disappointed and frustrated by this action. Henry would like him to publicly acknowledge that the idea originated with and was largely developed by Henry. Instead, he goes home and complains to his wife, who lacks the power to have his accomplishment recognized at work.

Henry needs to face this situation head-on. He should first ask his colleague for an appointment. When they meet, Henry needs to review his initial input to the project and his role in developing the concept. Since this is a business situation, he should report disappointment and frustration that his contribution was not recognized. He should avoid using terms such as *furious* or *disgusted* that would be likely to set his co-worker on edge. Henry should ask his co-worker to acknowledge his contribution in very specific terms to their boss: "I would like you to tell him that I initiated the idea of developing an online explanation of our benefits options and that I wrote the first sample section." Then he needs to end the conversation by saying that he values their working relationship. He hopes they can work together in the future, with each claiming credit for their own contributions to joint projects.

Choose carefully when to reveal your feelings in business situations. Even if he could find the courage to speak, Bill probably shouldn't tell his boss how annoyed he is at having to attend a national conference. At most, he might want to report frustration or hope for the future. "The Chicago conference is only a month after the Milwaukee meeting," he might say. "Both Fay and I are frustrated that I've been away so often. We're hoping my travel schedule will lighten up."

Speak from Personal Experience

Do you know anyone who is always blasting forth hot air? Chances are, this know-it-all is speaking in very grand, but vague, terms that have little to do with him. Often this type of person attempts to bark out orders, or maybe he speaks in such formless generalities that no one knows what the subject or point is.

On the other hand, while blathering, these people often presume to define the "right" way to see things. The catch is, there is no one *right* way. Everyone has a unique perspective, and each of us is the authority on precisely one: our own.

Here are some concrete examples to help you avoid sounding like a know-it-all.

- *The wrong way to voice an objection:* "There's no way we can get this report done in 2 days!"

- *The right way:* "The last time I did a profile like this, it took me 5 hours just to get the information I needed. Then it was another 3 days before I had a first draft. I don't think it's possible to get this written up in 2 days without more help."

Sharing all of the information you have helps your listener arrive at the same conclusion you've come to. Also, rather than creating another conflict, you're building a shared body of knowledge from which you can both draw possible solutions.

Bill's daughter Tory very much wants to go to an away football game, but he's withholding permission. Which of the following gives her a better chance of getting him to change his mind?

- *First version:* "Dad, you never let me do anything. I might as well be living in a prison! Everybody else but me has parents who care about their kids."

- *Second version:* "Dad, all my best friends—Samantha, Tameeka, Sam, Gloria, and even Priscilla—have permission from their parents to ride the school bus to the game next weekend. Today, Samantha and Tameeka spent all lunchtime talking about what they would wear and where they wanted to sit on the bus. The three of us were at the same table. I felt really out of it!"

Notice the way you felt about Tory after reading each version? Perhaps she won't be able to go on the trip, but her dad will no doubt give the matter serious consideration rather than reflexively responding "Tough!" as he may have to the first version.

Be Specific

Nothing makes a conversation sing more than specifics. Consider the following comment from a manager to her employee.

- *Wrong way:* "You've done a good job."

- *Right way:* "You've thoroughly covered the background and included relevant material from the Seemons project. Despite all the attention to background, you've still managed to come up with the original idea of direct e-mail to all their distributors. Good job!"

This manager knows that nothing is more energizing than close attention to our successes. Having received this kind of feedback, her employee knows not only that his efforts are valued but also what kinds of performance his manager sees as deserving of high praise. He is much more likely to try to maintain or repeat these conditions.

Specifics also help to bolster your credibility. During a meeting, Henry

> ## What Your Body Is Saying
>
> Clearly, it's not only what you say but also how you say it. Do your best to match what your words and body communicate by being aware of these body messages.
>
> - *Arms folded across the chest:* Suspicion and self-protection
> - *Tight facial and body muscles:* Suspicion and self-protection
> - *Torso leaning backward:* Suspicion and self-protection
> - *Torso leaning forward:* Interest
> - *Brow knitted:* Anger or other distress
> - *Corners of the mouth turned downward:* Sadness
> - *Corners of the mouth turned downward and taut:* Disgust
> - *Corners of the mouth turned slightly upward:* Enjoyment
> - *Wide-eyed expression and tight body:* Fear
> - *Lack of eye contact (except in Asian cultures):* Lack of interest
> - *Lax body:* Lack of interest

is asked for his opinion on a proposed new product. He replies that it sounds like a good idea, but despite all his knowledge on the subject, he leaves it at that.

Henry could list what he sees as the specific advantages and disadvantages and document each observation with the personal experiences or data that led to that conclusion: "The annual reports indicate sales of mobile communication equipment have gone up about 300 percent in the past 2 years, and our market research shows users are discarding their older models for newer versions once every 2½ years. Multifunctional devices are already on the market, but why give them this gold mine? I suggest we complete the development of our prototype on an accelerated schedule."

Henry's detailed answer makes his opinion much more authoritative and less dependent on the force of his personality. Instead of relying on his reputation, he's letting his specific words speak for themselves.

Send Appropriate Nonverbal Messages

What's the main characteristic that renders some speakers effective and others not? What makes some actors big stars and others forgettable? Chances are a big part of the difference is how they come across in ways that go beyond the content of what they're saying. And that's related to body language—how they look and sound when they say whatever it is that they have to say.

More than half of your message comes from the way you hold and move your body, your facial expressions, and the tone and volume of your voice. If the content of your words and the nonverbal messages you give don't agree, your listener will actually interpret your nonverbal messages as indicative of your true intention. Stating that you're disappointed while smiling broadly—or even looking deadpan—sends two conflicting messages. Saying softly that you plan to cooperate while your arms are crossed, your lips drawn, and your brow knitted confuses your listener at best. She'll probably conclude that you don't plan to cooperate at all. If you say, "It's so nice to see you!" while your lips are curled into a snarl, your conversational partner probably isn't going to see you as being very sincere.

Before you have to speak in a contentious or otherwise anxiety-provoking situation, take a deep breath, gather your thoughts, and quickly scan your body to notice any conflicting messages. And remember what your mom always said: Don't forget to smile (if the situation warrants it). The simple act of smiling can begin to change your body chemistry and make you feel more optimistic, and it will certainly have a beneficial effect on your audience.

Practice, Practice, Practice

Do our suggestions seem like a lot to keep straight all at once? They can be. But just as with any complex skill, such as driving or riding a bike, the independent actions start coming together and suddenly, you're off! In the beginning, focus on one suggestion at a time.

- When you're in conversation this coming week, practice speaking up.

- Write down any observations about your experience in your notebook. Take note of every time you consciously used any of our tactics and how doing it affected your feelings. Did you become more at ease or feel more confident?

- Next to each of these situations, note if it had an impact on your audience. Did people seem more receptive? Were they taken aback? Was your request honored more quickly than you'd expected?

MARGARET LEARNS TO SPEAK OUT

At first, Margaret needed to motivate herself. She had invested most of her life energy in her job but didn't quite appreciate yet the degree to which she was sabotaging her own success. She would have been deeply hurt if told she was being a lot less capable at work than she could be. Somehow she needed to realize that she could be more successful than she was.

Fortunately, Margaret became interested in a preconference workshop at an annual meeting. The title intrigued her: "Additional Verbal Weapons for Your Child Advocacy Arsenal." Margaret cared deeply about the children of her state. She knew what a difference programs such as early childhood education and improved reading courses could make. She was always on the lookout for ways to become a better advocate for children. If learning some new way of speaking would do it, she was all for it. So she enrolled.

The workshop leader was a younger woman who headed the education department in a large state. In addition to all the other ways in which this leader was a dynamo, she had learned years earlier how to speak effectively. Initially shy, she had taken several workshops and then forced herself to apply what she learned. In teaching this workshop, she shared her own odyssey. She once had a proposal that she had had trouble getting support for, until she learned to speak in ways that got her heard. Afterward, the department—and then the legislature—adopted the proposal.

This was a concept dear to Margaret's heart. From that point onward, Mar-

garet listened very carefully. From this role model, she began to understand the importance of just putting her ideas out there. After returning from the conference, Margaret enrolled in one of our workshops to improve her communication skills. The deep sense of modesty that had kept her from self-promoting began to dissipate. At both the national conference and during our workshop, she came to realize that "I" was not a dirty word.

Margaret made great strides, although it took her a while to develop her own style of dynamic communication. She was constantly on the lookout for good opportunities to share her ideas and her message. She listened carefully during conversations and then tailored her message to best communicate her perspective to each particular audience. In many ways, she had been a political whiz for years— she just never thought to use the same principles in conversation. But she knew the children were worth speaking up for, and this mission gave her the courage to stand up and be heard.

Much of Margaret's wish list for the children remained just that, but department members began listening to her. And one of her pet projects, which involved a program for early childhood education, was made law for the first time.

LEARN TO LISTEN

One of Margaret's strengths was that she listened well. This is easier for some of us than for others. The truth is that *everyone* needs to know how to listen well. You begin by letting the other person speak while you remain quiet. All you do is nod and look interested. Try to focus your attention on what is being said. This can help someone really open up to you. In addition, this person will be more likely to listen to you in the future. The result? An improved relationship!

Will Channing's impressive career began early. He was a scholarship student with a sports letter from Exeter. He was on the dean's list and in a social club at Harvard, where he earned an MBA. Upon graduation, he joined an international company and became a senior vice president by age 40.

Field Guide

THE BEDROOM

You and your husband, Richard, have been together for 4 years and married for the past 2, so you've had some time to discover that there are several differences in your sexual styles. But you haven't really discussed these differences.

You also love your warm flannel nightgowns for sleeping. You like the mystery of a dressed Richard—what's on can always come off, at appropriate times. Richard prefers a more open view—if he had his way, you would both sleep naked.

You love each other deeply and plan to stay married for your entire lives. What can you do to get more pleasure out of your sex life?

Communication is key here. Since you haven't had the best luck with effective communication during times of arousal, you're going to start by discussing your preferences and differences at another time. You and Richard talk about discussing lovemaking: Is it better to do that in bed or out? You know the setting should be relaxed, one where you'll have each other's complete attention, neither is tired, and you have plenty of time.

At the first discussion, you take the opportunity to talk about what you prefer, focusing only on what you like (and care-

At work, Will was regarded as a go-getter. Articulate, full of good ideas, and an effective supervisor, he managed an entire division. Profits had risen since he had taken over. Occasionally, people in the inner circle at the company observed that Will hadn't reached the top of his ladder quite yet!

fully avoiding talking about how you *don't* like some of Richard's turn-ons).

When it's Richard's turn, he says, "I like the sight of your naked body." That makes you feel great, and it's much better than if he said, "I get turned off when I can't see all of you." You both make "I" statements, describing your feelings and speaking from personal experience, listening carefully to each other, and avoiding judgments, questions, analysis, or advice. When you talk, you report; when you listen, you're just there to hear and absorb.

You use the same techniques for talking about everything from foreplay to the act itself. You find that the key is to stay open, not defensive. Encourage each other to follow thoughts all the way through, regardless of how awkward it may seem.

All of this communication has helped each of you articulate what you like. Now you have to figure out how to accommodate both perspectives in the same bed. Another skill to employ here is problem solving. That brainstorming session may be especially exciting! And if you keep it light and fun, you'll both be much happier.

Even if you didn't start out speaking skillfully, if you keep trying, you'll eventually speak this way naturally—at least when you aren't tired, hungry, or stressed out! (Under those circumstances, you may not have the energy to regulate your actions deliberately and may revert to your earlier habits.)

Tall and broad-shouldered, with an attractive smile, a light tan, and only a few gray strands among the blond hair around his temples, Will projected confidence. He was still in love with his wife, Betsy, with whom he shared three children. He considered himself blessed. Most aspects of his life had turned out as he had always hoped.

After five moves, Will's family lived in Greenwich, Connecticut. Their big 1920s Tudor sat on a grassy knoll that gently sloped down to a cove. A view of open water lay farther out, with the family's boat moored nearby. Behind their house were a cabana and a pool.

Despite these numerous riches, Will had a less than satisfying relationship with his son Thad. At 15, Thad seemed quite different from their two younger children (who were 6 and 8). He'd taken to answering questions in monosyllables. Whenever Will tried to talk to him, Thad shot him looks that conveyed indifference or impatience. Until about a year earlier, Will had made frequent efforts to communicate. Since then — as no topic appeared to capture Thad's interest — he tried less often.

From Will's perspective, Thad had it all. His parents were fully invested in his well-being and made an effort to spend time with him. He was encouraged in all his activities. Years ago, Will and Betsy had made a commitment that one or the other of them would attend all events their son participated in. Thad got to live at home. He attended a good school. He had a generous allowance. What more could a boy need?

In school, Thad had a B-minus average — not bad for a kid who cracked a book only during imposed study hours and stared into space much of that time. Mostly, Thad slouched on the sofa, glued to the classic movie channel on TV.

Once he got to high school, Thad was no longer interested in trying out for a sports team. He wasn't interested in the youth group at church — or much of anything else, as far as Will could tell.

Something needed to change. Will was in danger of losing whatever was left of a meaningful relationship with his son. What's more, Will worried that Thad wasn't connecting with anyone. He seemed to be adrift.

Will's motivation was clear-cut: He wanted to reconnect with his son. His business training enabled him to almost always think before acting. Confronted with any problem, he would ask, "Okay, what do I need to do to fix this?" His skills at assertion, problem solving, and saying no partly accounted for his spectacular rise in his company. In all these areas, he was in control. But as dad to a teen, he felt like a failure.

Will Needed to Listen to His Son

At work, Will met regularly with those directly beneath him. The people who reported to him knew that Will would pay attention and, if convinced of the need, make changes. During certain hours of the week, he had an open-door policy, and he was known as an excellent listener. Yet at home with his teenage son, he wasn't behaving this way.

Most parents of teens talk about having gaps in communication. Some parents are able to narrow this gap. They've learned to listen in a way that encourages their kids to talk—and sometimes even confide what's on their minds. Still, no one can deny that teenagers are their own breed. Many factors influence their behavior. These include power struggles between parent and teen, the teen's emerging sexuality, and the influence of peers—not to mention each teenager's own unique personality!

Will had taken the first move toward change by recognizing that his relationship with Thad was on a downward spiral. Their disagreements were definitely escalating: Will wanted curfews; Thad wanted none. Will believed doing chores builds character; Thad did them only after repeated nagging. Thad wanted to go on a camping trip to Maine with his friends; Will thought he shouldn't go. And wait—was that the odor of cigarettes on Thad's breath?

Sometimes Will found himself yelling at Thad, and Thad occasionally yelled back. More often, he simply shot Will a disgusted look. When Thad was at home, he spent most of his time in his room or watching TV.

Will had always done an admirable job of being accessible to his kids. But when Thad did communicate, Will would usually turn around and give him advice. He succumbed to the temptation to share his hard-won wisdom.

This strategy had worked for a long time with Thad. It still worked with the two younger children. But now Thad was a teenager. Will needed to adjust his parenting strategy to spend more time just listening. He needed to squelch his desire to interrupt. He might allow just an occasional "um-hmm," but nothing more. He needed to resist the urge to pontificate.

BE REALLY HERE

Take that old cliché seriously: You have two ears and one mouth for a reason! Listening helps you gather information. You learn the literal content of whatever the person is saying. You also may realize the underlying emotional message. By paying close attention, you will inevitably become a more knowledgeable person.

After listening carefully to someone else's perspective, you may realize that you actually agree with much of what has been said. And even if you choose to disagree, by repeating what you've heard the other person say, you'll let him know that you are open-minded. You haven't just dismissed his opinion without giving it any thought. This openness will buy you a lot of goodwill. If you've listened carefully, you're much more likely to have the opportunity to be listened to in turn. The net result? Solid communication that's truly about exchanging viewpoints. You're not just biding your time until you have a chance to speak. This kind of discussion is guaranteed to build bridges of understanding.

This week, we focused on speaking before listening. We believe it's very important that you value your own opinions. Give yourself and others the opportunity to know the real you. But that's only half of it. In order to have real connection, each person must speak and each must truly be there for the other—sending *and* receiving!

Teens are arguably the toughest crowd around. For that reason, they can probably teach us the most about effective communication. But several tactics can help, no matter whom you're speaking with.

Keep Quiet Until the Other Person Finishes

Sometimes the hardest part about listening is just keeping still. We're so geared up to accomplish something with every second of our lives. At times, you may feel wasteful or nonproductive when you just sit and lend someone your ear. Often we sit there *pretending* to listen when actually, we have a plan B up our sleeves, such as giving advice or talking about ourselves.

Let's eavesdrop on Tony and Marcia, just home from work. One snippet of conversation will reveal that their evening is unlikely to go well.

Tony begins, "I've had a really tough day at work. John was doing his usual number. I'm sure Bill knew what was going on, but I think he was looking the other way on purpose." He's about to continue, but he doesn't get a chance.

Marcia breaks in, "You think that's bad. You wouldn't believe my day . . ." and on and on she goes.

Tony feels belittled and annoyed. From her interruption, he's concluded that Marcia is not interested in him or in what he has to say about a topic that's important to him.

The discipline of keeping quiet until the other person is finished is both simple and anything but easy. While the other person is speaking, you may want to add information, ask questions, or offer advice. You may even be tempted to steer the conversation onto something about yourself. While this temptation is perfectly normal, resist it! Remain quiet, except for the occasional nod or "uh-huh."

Your ultimate goal is good *two-way* communication, but you'll best learn what the other person is thinking and feeling by allowing him to develop his own viewpoint fully. Eventually, you can take a turn speaking. Such mutuality will greatly increase the chance that each of you will feel connected to the other by the interchange.

Above all else, keep quiet! At first, your mind may wander. It's a bit like meditation in that way. Continually refocus on the other person's words, even as your mind strays. You may find other thoughts intruding. As you look the other person in the face, you may even find yourself thinking about her nose or skin. Gently try to bring your attention back to the content of what's being said. You may also begin to judge the other person. Stop and gently bring your attention back to the matter at hand. This process may repeat itself several times. Each time, take the focus off yourself. This includes avoiding observations that you aren't listening very well ("Oh, I've blown listening!"). Instead, refocus on the other person and what she's saying. This is not all about you!

Use Body Language That Shows Interest

Even before Marcia opened her mouth to steamroll over his story, Tony suspected that she wasn't very interested. She sat with her shoulders slumped, leaning back in her chair. He observed her looking down at her newly polished nails. Was he less important to her than "Pink Whisper" polish?

If you want the other person to think you value him, pay attention with your body, too. Just as when you're speaking, your listening body language needs to match your intent.

Most Americans and Europeans like a lot of eye contact, with the listener only occasionally looking away. In contrast, most Asians, as well as Native Americans, prefer less eye contact.

We're programmed to like a relaxed but attentive facial expression and body posture. Loosen your brow and jaw muscles. In a natural way, let your lips curl slightly upward. Settle your shoulders, uncross your arms, and lean slightly forward. Show the person that you feel alert, and nod if it works for you. An occasional "uh-huh" or an "uh-oh" may show that you're really listening and paying respectful attention.

For some people, this body language happens naturally, while others have to work at it. The next time you're in a conversation near a store window or a wall of mirrors, sneak a quick peek at your stance. Are your arms crossed or open? Are you leaning forward or back? All of these poses indicate your level of interest. Are they saying what you want them to say?

Reflect Back What the Other Person Says

Even a mannequin can look interested in what you have to say for a little while. The proof that you were *really* listening comes when you tell the other person what they've just said. Nothing is a more accurate signal of how well you were paying attention.

Eventually, the speaker will finish. It may take a few seconds or an eternity, but if you didn't interrupt, chances are good that he will be grateful for having a chance to complete a thought! Now, just summarize.

You can focus on what was said: "It sounds like your boss was out to lunch, so you got stuck with most of the work. You were working really hard all those hours!"

Or you may choose to focus on the feelings instead: "It seems like you're really put out that your boss lets all the work fall on you!"

Most important, don't add information, don't ask questions, and don't comment on what you think is good or bad about what you heard. Especially, don't give advice. At most, if you need to feel useful, just say, "How can I be of help?" rather than "You need to stand up to Bill. You need to tell him you'll quit unless he does a better job of supervising." If the other person wants your assistance, hopefully he'll tell you what would be really useful. The truth is that unless it's asked for, advice is rarely helpful. Unsolicited advice is in fact criticism.

In training people to be better listeners, we've found the following exercise particularly effective.

- After two people pair up, one speaks for an agreed-upon time (5 minutes is about right).

- Then the other person *only* reflects back what was said for 2 minutes. (Remember your skill of effective listening!)

- The first speaker has 1 minute to clear up any misunderstanding or say more.

- The participants then switch roles: The first speaker becomes the listener, and the first listener becomes the speaker. The same time limits and rules apply.

When it's your turn to speak, choose a topic that excites you. If your listener is your spouse or a good friend, you'll need to choose carefully in order to cover new ground. If you decide to discuss something contentious, start with a topic of *small* disagreement. You can work up to greater controversy on later occasions.

When you've chosen to discuss something controversial, after an initial round of speaking and listening, you have two options. You can either have other rounds right away or agree to return to the topic at a predetermined time the next day, with no further discussion until then. When you meet again, observe the same format as on the first day.

With contentious issues, we've found that whenever you finish as many rounds as needed to get everything said, you may still disagree, but at least you understand the other person. And you know that you've been heard, too.

Note that this structure makes it harder to turn a disagreement into a full-fledged argument. We encourage our workshop participants to try this exercise at home with someone they're close to. We're amazed at all the good reports we get.

- "I can't believe we discussed money and didn't argue!"
- "You know, after we really listened to each other, Lee and I found we had at least a few areas of agreement."
- "It's so simple. What an improvement! It's almost like our honeymoon all over again."
- "We didn't agree, but we were able to compromise. For us, that's great!
- "For once, my son didn't tune me out."

Be Prepared to Be Changed By What You Hear

The heart of the matter is that really listening may change you. An open attitude doesn't mean that you must change; it simply means that you're receptive to the possibility.

The Center for Creative Leadership, with campuses in North Carolina, Colorado, California, and Belgium, provides training to many top executives who come to one of their campuses for weeklong stays. Some of their programs are for top-flight administrators or executives in danger of becoming stalled in their careers or even let go. The center reports that one of the main characteristics of executives who derail is *rigidity*—the inability to adapt their style to change or to take feedback, listen, and learn. The ability to remain open to being changed by what you hear is the exact opposite of rigidity.

Try this at home, too. Really listening with an open mind can increase your closeness with your partner and especially with your teenagers. Make yourself available. Quiet attention usually works better with teens than giving them advice.

Sometimes, if you hang around long enough, they'll open up and even let you in on something that's bothering them. If they do report a problem, hold your tongue and remember to simply listen at first, and then reflect back. At most, say, "How can I be of help?" Sometimes the answer will be, "You have been, by listening."

If you're feeling brave, you might even attempt genuine listening with someone whose political opinions differ from yours. If you're able to do this successfully without creating unnecessary conflict, the other person may be willing to listen to you in turn. Who knows? The two of you may even discover a point of agreement—startling, but entirely possible with good listening.

In your notebook, write down these exercises and practice them during this week.

1. Choose one or more people with whom you have regular contact. Try listening along the lines suggested here. Observe afterward how effective this contact has been. Did you learn anything? Did the other person seem more relaxed and open? Did you? How did it feel to relax into the moment? Were you panicky? At ease? Frustrated? Surprisingly fulfilled?

2. Sometime during the week—whether you're in a coffee shop, at a restaurant, or near two of your co-workers—watch as two people converse. Note how well or ineffectively they listen, using the steps in this chapter. Are they talking over each other? Interrupting? How is their body language? Are they facing each other? Are their stances defensive, with arms crossed? Do they appear to be hearing and understanding?

3. Go back and look at previous entries in your Thoughts and Feelings Log. Would careful listening have helped you avoid any of those situations altogether?

Speaking and listening well, along with empathy, are the most effective tools we have to resolve differences. Bear in mind that your long-term relationships have a lot of points of contact. There are bound to be little areas where your beliefs are going to collide with someone else's. These relationships have to endure a lot of wear and tear over the course of a lifetime. Why not make the edges a bit smoother with some active, fully committed communication? You'll certainly enrich your relationships and your lives together by increasing your understanding of each other's beliefs and motives. At the very least, you'll trade some of your all-out arguments for some minor disagreements, which can make the long haul a bit less rocky.

WILL LEARNS TO LISTEN ACTIVELY

For a long time, Will thought his active listening wasn't succeeding. Thad still wasn't saying anything. Then one night, Thad began to complain about a Spanish test that had been put off after he had already studied. Will was tempted to get some more information so he could tell Thad what to do, but he resisted. Instead, he just said, "So Mr. Jones announced a test, you studied, and then the day before the test he told the class that the test wouldn't be given until the end of the week. After you put so much effort into preparing!"

Will noticed that his son looked at him sharply; previously, he had been staring into space. Thad didn't say anything, but his body language spoke for him: "You've really heard what I had to say. You aren't judging me in a way I need to protect myself against." For the rest of the time they were together that day, Thad seemed less on guard.

For years, Will had been the wise one and Thad the learner. That was still usually the case, but Will made great progress in his relationship with Thad when he really listened openly to his son's point of view. Sometimes Will was changed by what he heard, sometimes not. Once Thad knew that he could sometimes persuade his father to change a dictum, he became more invested in sharing his life with him.

By actively listening without reaching for his fatherly advice, Will was trying to encourage Thad to share his real self. Will came to know his son much better — not the little boy he once was or the man he would become, but the confused, mercurial, unsure, exploring person of the present, full of dreams and fears that he was only occasionally able to articulate, even to himself.

Will made sure to be around his son for a half hour or so each day. They usually shared a few moments together before the dinner hour as Thad ate a snack in the family room. Will kept mostly quiet on those occasions. When Thad did say something, Will listened attentively. As hard as it was, he resisted the temptation to treat the conversation as an information-gathering session. He also avoided responding as if he were issuing a policy directive to a subordinate.

Thad began to speak up about small matters, like what a crummy teacher Mr. Jones was. (Will found himself beginning to understand why Spanish wasn't Thad's favorite subject.) Thad also reported on the musical style of a favorite rock group on their latest CD, commented that the Constitutional Convention had been composed mainly of rich guys, and observed that trips to the Caribbean were available at rock-bottom prices in late spring. For about 2 months, Will got such input and quietly listened. Once Thad had finished, Will reflected back only what he had heard. They averaged about two conversations a week, and Thad was spending slightly less time in his room.

Then the family went for a boat ride one Sunday. Father and son walked along the rocky shore of an island and talked. When the subject of films somehow came up, Thad's whole expression changed as he talked animatedly about different movies. Will did his now-usual listening. To his amazement, Thad talked on and on.

Will arranged a similar outing for the following Sunday. This time, Thad confided his hopes for his future to his dad. What he really wanted to do was be involved in filmmaking. This led to other conversations on other Sundays about how best to prepare.

On his own, with the help of the guidance counselor at his school, Thad had checked out college programs that taught filmmaking. To get into an excellent program at a school like Southern Cal or New York University, he needed good grades. His grades didn't completely turn around overnight, but motivated by this information, Thad started taking more of an interest.

He also continued talking to Will, usually about filmmaking. But sometimes he'd make comments about what meatheads the high school jocks were or muse about whether he should ask the pretty girl with the great laugh to an upcoming party at a friend's house. ("Suppose she says no?") Regarding Thad's budding interest in girls, Will really had to use control to stifle his impulse to give advice, but his rational self realized that if his son wanted advice, he would ask for it.

After working on learning to be a better listener, Will felt that he knew his son. Will Channing—once again in control!

Week 6 Recap

Speaking

1. Just do it—speak up for the right amount of time.

2. Make "I" statements.

3. Report your feelings, when appropriate.

4. Speak from personal experience.

5. Be specific.

6. Send appropriate nonverbal messages.

Listening

1. Keep quiet while the other person is speaking.

2. Use body language that shows your interest in what is being said.

3. When the other person finishes speaking, reflect back the literal or emotional content of what you heard. Don't add information, interrogate, judge, or offer advice.

4. Be prepared to be changed by what you hear.

To improve both sides of communication, practice, practice, practice!

CHAPTER 9

WEEK 7: EMPATHIZE WITH OTHERS

Empathy is the act of seeing the world from the perspective of another person. You try to be aware of and appreciate why that person is acting or feeling in a particular way. After doing this, you may or may not agree with or accept that point of view. If you do decide to speak, you will understand better than before how best to approach this person.

Sharon Hedgepath dressed neatly and attractively in crisp blouses and A-line skirts. She made a habit of watching her diet and kept her petite body trim. In the morning, she applied just a smidgen of makeup to enhance her brown eyes and golden brown skin. All in all, Sharon looked quite pretty, which helped give others a good first impression.

As a wife, mother, and grandmother, Sharon was also blessed with many potential sources of social support. She was well positioned professionally as a research coordinator for a cardiac rehabilitation study at a major medical center, responsible for recruiting subjects, monitoring tests, and compiling data. Fortunately, her high intelligence and attention to detail ensured that she was up to the task.

To a casual observer, Sharon seemed to have a good life. Yet she wasn't happy. This became obvious after spending a few minutes in her company and looking at her body language. Sharon's characteristic stance at work and at home was with her arms crossed gracefully but firmly in front of her chest. She felt she was perpetually surrounded by jerks. At least she was standing up to them!

Because she knew her stress level was too high, Sharon came to us for coping skills training. A bright, articulate woman who knew the risks of her behavior, she realized she needed to get out of her rut. "I like a lot about my job: being left largely on my own; having contact with patients; knowing our study will expand knowledge of what really succeeds in cardiac rehab," she told us. "But I work with some very difficult personalities. The cardiologists demand a lot from me. If they try to tell me what's going on, they don't really know how to communicate well. Some never bother to try. And some of the rehab specialists aren't much better."

Her biggest irritation was a co-worker, Janet, with whom she had shared an office. Janet had moved out when she was promoted, and she now held a position higher than Sharon's. The two weren't getting along, that much was clear. Although Sharon had absolutely no designs on Janet's job, she thought Janet might still think of her as a threat because she had more education.

The biggest source of conflict, according to Sharon, were the 30 binders belonging to Janet that still overflowed from the bookcases in Sharon's office. She had asked Janet to remove them, and Janet had retorted that Sharon could do it herself. When we asked if Sharon would consider doing this, she said, "Never! It's out of the question. I wouldn't give that you-know-what an inch!"

Sharon often thought about switching to another department in the medical center, yet she realized that a different position would come with its own set of problems. Still, she really didn't like working with this woman.

To compound her problems, Sharon told us, her retired husband, Howard, had recently acted like a jerk. The 3-year-old who lived next door had just gotten a tricycle. Sharon came home to find that Howard had finished a roll of film in their camera with eight shots of this child learning to ride his tricycle. She had planned on finishing that roll on an upcoming trip. One photo, she could see. But eight?

She'd certainly let Howard know what she thought of that. "He is cute," she

admitted, "but we don't know him that well. You're always taking all these mul-
tiple shots! Didn't you think?"

When asked how the rest of the evening had gone, she replied, "Badly!" What
had she accomplished by telling him off? "Nothing, really," she admitted. "I
stomped off to do the laundry, and he stomped off to the kitchen to fix dinner.
Through bedtime, we didn't speak much."

To put it mildly, Sharon wasn't feeling warm and fuzzy toward her co-workers
or her husband. Instead, a free-floating sense of alienation reigned. Her daughter
and granddaughter lived some distance away, so Sharon spent most of her time
among people from whom she often felt estranged. She was also not one to cultivate
a lot of hobbies or invest the time in growing close to other friends. In order to be-
come happy, Sharon needed to learn how to improve her key relationships.

Sharon Needed to See Different Perspectives

Sharon knew something had to change, but she wasn't quite sure what. Then she
saw a flyer we'd posted to attract subjects to our research study measuring the ef-
fects of training. It read, "Is Stress at Home or Work Getting to You?" She figured
she didn't have anything to lose, so she called to volunteer. We were looking for
people with slightly elevated scores for anxiety, depression, hostility, or perceived
stress or slightly low scores on social support—which certainly described Sharon.
By the luck of the draw, Sharon was randomly assigned to the group that received
training instead of the waiting list control group.

Sharon proved to be a prolific record keeper, writing up several situations each
day as log entries. In each one, she put down full paragraphs of negative thoughts.
She also recorded her feelings with great precision. Sticking to the objectively
observable facts of a given situation proved more difficult, since Sharon had a ten-
dency to add her own interpretations of situations, seeing them as fact.

When she first began to ask the I AM WORTH IT questions, she replied
quickly. Of course, her negative reactions were justifiable! It was appropriate to
be very angry that the binders were still in her office. It was appropriate to be dis-
gusted that her husband had used up the rest of the film on pictures of the little boy.

And so it went whenever she asked the I AM WORTH IT questions, log entry after log entry.

During the course of her training, Sharon began to observe that she always assumed from the start that her reaction was appropriate. In fact, she saw that she believed, by definition, that her perspective was the only possibility. What she wanted was a proper solution to what she saw as the constant problem: the misbehavior of others. She was in the right; they were in the wrong.

In reality, matters often weren't so simple, but in order to be able to come to that realization, Sharon needed to learn to practice empathy.

READ OTHERS

You need on occasion to be able to persuade someone else of the wisdom of your words. To truly be in control, you need also to have the ability to get along with nearly everyone, even difficult personalities. As you probably already know from experience, it's best to avoid having these kinds of people dig in their heels.

Empathy is one of the most powerful strategies in this book. You'll be amazed at how much more you're able to accomplish if you just begin to make a habit of appreciating the other person's point of view.

Know that empathy at home helps relationships. Tom and Cynthia, who've been married for a number of years, haven't learned to practice empathy. If they both acquired this skill, their relationship could be much improved, but instead, on this Saturday morning, they spiral downward.

Tom learns that friends have offered to give him their tickets for this afternoon's hockey game. He tells Cynthia. She responds by saying that she had plans for them to go shopping. Tom is puzzled and disappointed.

Tom needs to figure out Cynthia's point of view. She thinks that the money she'll save on a bargain item will mean they'll have more money for the down payment on a house they've been saving for. But Tom doesn't grasp this; he simply concludes that Cynthia is fickle and selfish.

On the flip side, Tom really likes sports. They remind him of his younger days as a star athlete. Games provide one of the few occasions when he can relax completely and yell *for* something. Usually when he yells, it's against! Without understanding this perspective, Cynthia concludes that Tom is rigid and unappreciative and that he is selfish for still insisting on attending the game.

It's likely that no matter how well they might have understood each other, Cynthia and Tom would have had different viewpoints. But if each had tried to understand the other's perspective, they probably would have more mutual respect. Maybe they needed to flip a coin. Or maybe Tom could have attended the game, and Cynthia could have gone shopping. Either way, appreciating each other's point of view would possibly lead to a better outcome.

Know that empathy helps at work, too. Traditionally, workplace differences were related to age, social class, ethnicity, or religion. Now some of us need to get along with foreign employees, vendors, customers, and bosses. International associates may structure dealings differently. Even what's considered important may be different. Without awareness of and respect for such differences, relationships may falter. Let's look at how globalization affected business students at one college campus.

Every Friday afternoon, the Fuqua School of Business at Duke University hosts a social gathering. Students in the masters programs come together on "Fuqua Friday" to drink beer or soda, snack, and talk. Spouses are invited, too. Early in the first semester of the 2-year program, these contacts expand the students' acquaintance circles, since many are new to the campus. It's especially important to the one-third of students who have just arrived from other countries, as they usually have even fewer social contacts.

Ana Lucia Melo and her husband had arrived in the United States 2 months ago. They mingled mainly with other Brazilians and the few Americans they knew. In Brazil, when people are introduced, it's customary for women to kiss men and women on both cheeks. Men give women the same greeting. Ana had continued this custom here and had always been treated warmly when she did so.

At her first Fuqua Friday gathering, Ana was introduced to fellow student Devendra Gupta from India. She gave him her usual social greeting. His wife, Parima, was quite taken aback and deeply offended. How dare Ana engage in such a brazen gesture—and right in front of her, too! After much explaining, Parima was persuaded that this gesture did not have the meaning she attached to it. Another lesson learned as an essential part of business school training.

Do another person's averted eyes mean that he is on guard or being respectful? Does camaraderie mean you have a deal, or is that just the way businessmen in that country always act? Is a gesture made by a male colleague as inappropriate in his culture as it is in yours? Are the minutes of socializing at the beginning of a meeting considered a waste of time or a conventional first-stage icebreaker? Learning empathy can help you decipher everything—from which considerations will be most important in decision making to how the power structure of a particular organization can influence its future. In other words, empathy is a critical business skill, and not just in the international realm.

Like listening, empathy always improves results. Sometimes the only reason to use empathy is to make a good thing better. Let's say you recognize that someone really went out of his way for you. Perhaps his efforts represented a bigger commitment of time or money or involved greater personal sacrifice than you initially realized. By taking a moment to say, "I'll bet working overtime [or baking 15 dozen cookies or saying you're sorry] wasn't easy, and I appreciate your efforts in doing that," you've put the icing on an already wonderful situation and solidified the possibility of something similar happening in the future.

Other times, you may want to use an empathy exercise because you're experiencing a negative feeling and want to understand the other person's motives *before* asking the I AM WORTH IT questions. Understanding that person's behavior from his own perspective—and, in some cases, why he saw his behavior as positive—can be especially helpful in deciding whether your initial reaction was appropriate and if taking action is worth it. Once you have that information, you can choose between acceptance and assertion. Basically, empathy can boost the power of the I AM WORTH IT questions—and your ability to have the situation resolved the way you'd like.

Remember to Listen

This week's exercises build on last week's listening skill. Start by learning what the other person is thinking and feeling. Often you can accomplish this simply by seeking out his company and listening with an open mind. Ask open-ended questions as needed. Sometimes you will need to ask a third party or do a little background reading to get a firm handle on the subject.

Often, our idea of what will relax, stimulate, or threaten someone proves to be wrong. A person's dreams and fears can be very different than we imagine.

The first thing Tom and Cynthia needed was to understand the point of view of the other. Tom may not have appreciated how important the down payment fund was to Cynthia. Cynthia may not have appreciated the importance of the hockey game to Tom. They could have learned this by listening.

Let's take another example. Say your teenager answers you sullenly, with an "uh-huh." Instead of jumping down his throat and scolding him about his attitude, maybe you need to listen first. Perhaps you'll find out that he flunked a test, wasn't invited to a party, didn't get the part-time job he wanted, or didn't make the team. If you find out any of this, the "uh-huh" may become more understandable, especially if you remember how important these matters were when you were that age. Here's what you may find out if you listen.

You: "How was your day?"

Your teen: "Okay." (He doesn't look you in the eye and has a sullen expression on his face.)

You: "Okay, huh?"

Your teen: "Yeah. Smith gave a pop quiz. I hadn't done the reading."

You: "Sounds tough!"

Your teen: "Yeah."

Practice this empathy exercise this week. Choose a problem you're having with another person. It could involve either an ongoing irritation that you experience as a result of a frequent, particular behavior on the part of that person or simply a difference of opinion. In your notebook, describe the problem from your point of view. Use "I" statements to describe your thoughts and feelings: "I am annoyed that in our current budget crunch, Ken still wants to hold the big meeting at a resort instead of at the office."

Next, seek out and truly listen to the other person to learn as much as you can about how he sees the problem you've chosen: "Ken, as you know, you and I are having some differences of opinion about whether to hold the big meeting here or at a resort. Before I mull this over any further, it would be helpful if you could explain to me again all the reasons you prefer the resort setting."

Record the results in your notebook, then move on to the next tactic for empathy.

Know That Others Also See Themselves as Good and Right

Most people think they are basically good, doing their best to make the world a better place. How do they arrive at that conclusion?

After listening to someone tell you her perspective, it's often helpful to try to pretend that you are that person. Use "I" statements. How does the situation look from another viewpoint?

If Tom and Cynthia had done this, Tom first would have listened to

Cynthia. Then he would have imagined what Cynthia was thinking: "I'm helping the family to get a house."

Cynthia would also have listened to Tom, so she needed to get into his shoes and imagine what he was thinking: "I am sure that this will be a great family outing. After all, sports events are the most enjoyable thing a family can do together!"

If this couple had taken the time to listen and then empathize, they could have appreciated each other's point of view, and their argument would have been less likely to erupt. You can also use this technique to understand those with whom you disagree—but have no interest in ever speaking with—in order to eliminate the negative energy of disagreeing from your body.

Suppose Mr. Jones doesn't want to support the bond issue to build what, in your view, are critical additional classrooms for your child's school. You decide not to speak to him about it, but you'd like to stop harboring so many negative thoughts about him. You think: "Mr. Jones's taxes have gone up with each new 5-year evaluation, but his income hasn't. Maybe he's worried about whether he'll have enough money when he retires in a few years." Or maybe it's: "Mr. Jones is overextended by his bigger house payments. He's probably squeezed too tight right now to be thinking about much else."

Working further on the situation from the previous empathy exercise, describe the difference of opinion from the other person's point of view. Try to put yourself in his shoes. Imagine the favorable light in which he sees himself. How does he justify his position on the problem in question? Use "I" statements to describe his viewpoint.

Assuming Ken's perspective about the resort meeting, our example might go like this. "Our big meetings are opportunities to energize and galvanize our sales force. These meetings are usually held at a resort. If we deviate from that this year, we'll underline the financial crunch. It will dramatically drive home the fact that sales are down. This is likely to further discourage everybody. I can make everyone leave that meeting feeling upbeat—but only if I'm given our usual setting. I'm being held partly responsible. It's only fair that I be given the resources to do my job properly.

"On a more personal note, keeping sales up is my responsibility. I'm concerned that I already look bad. If sales decline even more, I'm going to look even worse!"

Sometimes you may need to appreciate how important the matter is to someone else. Only then might you realize that the other person is much more invested in this issue than you are, and you may decide it's best for everyone if you acquiesce. If you choose instead to persevere, you're more likely to get what you want if you can acknowledge any sacrifice that your request represents on the other person's part.

Decide between Acceptance and Assertion

Perhaps the most powerful use of empathy is to help you decide between accepting the situation and asserting yourself in order to change it. Once you've mastered the I AM WORTH IT questions and have made it a habit to stop and evaluate your own feelings, you can take a moment to employ empathy *before* you ask yourself the four questions. This extra step may take you in a completely new direction, and it will certainly make it easier for you to decide if you want to ask the person to alter a behavior or if you can just accept it. If you decide to ask for a change by practicing assertion, how can you use empathy in your request?

Let's say you're running late for work and a morning meeting. You can feel yourself getting upset and anxious, and it's pretty clear why. You take the extra step of empathy to ask yourself, "How will this affect my colleagues?" Your answer inspires you to call and let your supervisor and co-workers know that you understand how this will affect them and then to employ assertion to be sure your work is done correctly.

- *Objective facts:* "It's 8:10 now and the traffic has been stalled for quite a while just before the bridge. I'm going to be late."

Coaching Yourself

When you do your empathy exercises, it's likely that no one will
be prodding you with questions. If you run out of ideas about
what the person you have chosen to empathize with would say
next, consider whether the following questions would be appropriate to ask yourself.

• What is his home life typically like? Are there any special challenges there?

• Are there any areas of work or other interests that he is especially invested in?

• Does he have any particular vulnerabilities?

• What is it about himself that he is especially proud of?

These questions will help you home in on the core issues that
this person struggles with, as well as his primary motivations.
Use this information to help increase your empathy for him and
thereby improve your communication with each other.

• *Empathetic acknowledgment:* "I realize this inconveniences everybody
in the meeting and makes it more difficult for you to be sure I've
caught everything, unless you repeat it all when I arrive."

• *Requests:* "Perhaps my presentation could be moved to a later slot on
the agenda. And I'll call Matt and ask him to explain the situation to
the others and take notes on what I'll be missing."

Or perhaps you need to get a co-worker to finish a job. As you practice assertion, how are you going to acknowledge that person's point of view?

• *Objective facts:* "I've unloaded three boxes."

• *Feelings:* "I'm getting really tired of boxes."

- *Empathetic acknowledgment:* "I know you much prefer to be out on the floor, dealing with customers."

- *Request:* "Still, I need to ask you to unload the next two boxes to give me a break. Okay?"

Or maybe you need to ask your partner to take her turn putting the kids to bed. After all, you're tired, too.

- *Objective facts:* "Honey, it's your turn to put the kids to bed."

- *Empathetic acknowledgment:* "I know you've had a really tough day."

- *More objective facts:* "I had to work through my lunch break myself."

- *More empathetic acknowledgment and request:* "I know it can be a challenge to get them to sleep, but I need you to take your turn."

Consider a situation that you've previously listed in your notebook. Decide whether you want to ask the person to change or if you'll agree to disagree. If you'd like to request a change, write your plan very specifically. What exactly will you say to let the person know you understand where she's coming from *and* that you'd like to ask her for a change? On the other hand, if you decide to accept the person and the situation, write down why you've chosen acceptance.

Try repeating this entire writing exercise this week with another person and another bothersome behavior. Begin by listening and gathering any other needed information and follow up by empathizing, then decide between acceptance and assertion. At first, you may find yourself practicing empathy only as an intellectual exercise, especially in minor situations where you'll never have much information about the other person. This can be a bit of fun and good training for real empathy, because developing a capacity to view multiple perspectives is a useful skill. How does the person who sped through the intersection at the end of the yellow light see his action? Why would your daughter's teacher assign a big test 2 days after spring break?

Use these just as practice—don't substitute them completely for the very real learning opportunities for real empathy, in which you find out the facts and remain open to appreciating the perspective of the other party. This skill is like a muscle: The more you work with it, the stronger it will become and the easier it will be to use all your other muscles (or skills) as a result.

SHARON LEARNS TO APPRECIATE OTHER PERSPECTIVES

By learning to be empathetic, Sharon achieved breakthroughs in two troubled relationships. As part of her training, she was asked to assume the role of her co-worker Janet and describe how she felt when Sharon requested that she remove the binders that were filling the bookcases.

"Every day for the past few weeks, I have been glued to this desk. . . . I have this big deadline," Sharon said, as she tried to assume the identity of Janet.

"Anything more, Janet?" we asked Sharon.

"I feel a lot of pressure about that, especially with the promotion. I don't have time to think about the binders. And frankly, I don't have the energy, either," she admitted.

"Anything else?"

"Storage is difficult. My office is filled with new stuff. It may require reorganizing the whole storage closet—a huge job!"

Sharon was surprised by this projection exercise. The question of what to do with the binders looked very different from Janet's perspective. Sharon's negative feelings weren't about Janet but about the binders that were still in her office.

Then she was ready to approach Janet. "I realize you're really busy right now," she said. "And I know finding a place to store the binders is quite a hassle." She then asked for Janet's help in figuring out a solution. Janet was receptive but explained that she needed to finish a major project with an impending deadline before she could think about the binders.

Sharon and Janet still have to deal with the storage problem, but Sharon's empathetic overtures have established an attitude that's much more likely to result in a solution to their common dilemma.

Next, Sharon turned her attention to Howard. The following weekend, when she visited her daughter and granddaughter in Illinois, Sharon had planned to shoot the rest of the film and have the pictures developed there. She was encouraged to practice empathy toward Howard when it was her turn next in our workshop.

"Pretend to be Howard and then tell us why you took those pictures of the neighbor's child," we said.

"Okay. Now I'm Howard. I'm just not very talented with cameras."

"Do you think Howard would see it that way? Does Howard like taking pictures?" we asked.

"Yes, he likes that a lot."

"If it's a favorite pastime of his, do you think he sees himself as lacking talent?"

"No, I suppose not," Sharon replied.

"How do you think taking pictures of the 3-year-old fits in to his attitude toward taking pictures?" we prodded.

"I suppose he imagines himself a photographer. Maybe he thinks these shots will become part of his portfolio."

"Can you think of anything else that might affect his attitude?"

"Perhaps it would be a gesture toward the neighbor, like taking her a pie or something," she speculated. "Yes, I think he might consider that."

"That's showing a lot of empathy. Now turn your attention back to the roll of film."

When Sharon thought about it, she began to see that she wanted her husband to take the finished roll to a store with 1-hour developing and get a new roll. Assuming his perspective, she began, "I know you like taking pictures, and the little boy is cute." She then asked him for what she needed.

Looking at it from this perspective, Sharon could clearly see how the scenario she had just role-played would probably have led to a better outcome with her husband.

These empathy exercises caused a breakthrough for Sharon. Eventually, she began to relax her body language. She started to realize that perhaps she had been a bit rigid, and the end result had often made the real stressors worse.

"I knew all of this already, really. My husband and I were in counseling together a few years ago," she confessed. "I know I'm supposed to see other perspectives. I started out that way, but I've drifted. Gradually, practicing what I knew began to feel like too much trouble. And as day-to-day life got worse, I didn't have the energy to try. But I can see I need to go back to practicing."

"Why is that?" we asked.

"Because my life goes a lot better when I do!"

Week 7 Recap

1. Begin by listening to learn as much as possible about the other person.

2. Try to temporarily assume her identity, to see the world through her eyes. She likely sees herself as a good person making the world a better place. How does she arrive at that conclusion?

3. Once you appreciate where the other person is coming from, decide between acceptance and assertion.

CHAPTER 10

WEEK 8: LEARN TO LOOK UP

Some people seem to have positive experiences most of the time. This week, you'll learn strategies to help you get there, too. You'll learn ways to have your positive remarks far outweigh criticisms when dealing with others. You'll learn to look for the optimistic aspects of most situations you find yourself in, and how to think about yourself in a way that's upbeat.

Arnold Marone taught English at a high school in a suburb along the shoreline of Lake Michigan, just north of Chicago. Round-faced and bald, he had the some-what droopy body of a scholar. He could be a bit dour: His relatives bored him; his neighbors didn't keep up their properties; and he felt sure our culture was in a decline. In most areas of his life, he managed to find a thing or two to complain about. But when the subject was Highland Park High School or British writers, Arnold oozed enthusiasm, for he was devoted to both.

Indeed, Arnold's life revolved around his teaching. He always directed the annual school play, even though it involved many afternoons and evenings of rehearsals. He usually gave essay tests instead of multiple choice or fill-in-the-blank exams, even though essays took a lot longer to grade. He read works of crit-icism to prepare for his classes.

Arnold had attended night school and summer classes a number of years earlier. He had finally received a Master of Arts in English literature from the University of Illinois at Chicago. The degree got him a job at Highland Park soon afterward. Now he hoped to be the next head of the English department, once the present chair retired. Arnold also dreamed of having the yearbook dedicated to him. Alas, in all his 20 years at Highland Park, it had never happened, although several other English teachers had received the honor.

A longtime bachelor, Arnold was unlikely to ever marry. He liked his world to be orderly and predictable. He had almost proposed to a woman 20 years earlier, but then decided he didn't want to live with someone who was nearly always late. Another relationship had blossomed for a while a decade later, but Arnold decided that woman talked too much. Now 47, with a diminished sex drive, he was content to devote himself to teaching and bonding with his dog, a standard poodle.

The year we met him, the present chairman, Charles, a genial man, was pre-occupied with creating a new curriculum for the 10th-grade course on American writers. He offered Arnold the opportunity to teach the senior advanced-placement English course. Arnold was thrilled. These were the best humanities students in a very bright student body. Over the past decade, students from the honors section had gone on to study at the University of Chicago, Harvard, Yale, Princeton, Duke, and many other top schools.

Because all the honors students aspired to attend highly competitive colleges, senior year was stressful. The grades and recommendations Arnold gave them could affect their chances of being admitted to their schools of choice. In turn, how well Arnold performed as their teacher might affect his chance of becoming the next department head.

He was determined to demonstrate that he was up to his new assignment. In addition to the standard readings, he decided to supplement the course with a written critical essay, due every 3 weeks. He announced at the beginning of the year that any paper with more than two words or phrases that didn't conform to either the Chicago Manual of Style or the rules of standard English usage would auto-matically receive, at best, a C.

The class, which covered British literature from the works of Shelley to those of more contemporary writers, began well enough. Most of these bright students liked reading Shelley and Keats. Then the first round of 500-word papers was turned in. In an essay of more than 1,000 words, Sean, one of the brightest students in the class, argued against the key idea in Keats's "Ode on a Grecian Urn." Arnold found five glaring grammar mistakes and gave the essay a C. Sean, who had formerly been a sparkplug in class, didn't seem to have much to say after he got his paper back.

In class, Arnold applied skills that he had honed in graduate school. What was the flaw in the argument? What conditionals needed to be attached? At first, only a few of the students appeared to get the idea, but gradually, more were catching on. Arnold noticed, though, that perhaps one-third to one-half of the students responded only when called upon. Their answers were correct, but they seemed to be saying as little as possible. Clearly, this class wasn't providing the students with the riveting experience he had hoped for.

No doubt, Arnold was succeeding in teaching his students the rules of grammar. Their speech and writing were becoming more well-structured and precise, but he was failing in his bigger goal of getting them excited about English literature.

Arnold Needed to Be Less Negative

At the beginning of the 12th-grade English curriculum report, the chairman had listed the course's goals:

- To inspire each student to want to read on his or her own more of the works of at least one of the authors studied

- To expose students to times, places, and situations previously beyond their ken

- To familiarize students with the history of British writers

- To familiarize students with the guidelines of standard English usage

The first three goals place almost exclusive emphasis on the positive. Arnold was focusing almost exclusively on the fourth, which is more mixed. Even within that, he was stressing what not to do rather than what would convey the students' ideas most effectively.

If he had thought about it earlier, Arnold would have realized that his own goals were about the same as those listed in the curriculum, and in the same order. But he was failing to align his teaching style with his aspirations.

Why was Arnold placing so much emphasis on the negative? Perhaps he felt a bit threatened by students who were as bright or brighter than he. Perhaps his teaching style was a reflection of his dour nature. Maybe he was emulating his own professors. Maybe it was just easier to focus on objective criteria, such as grammar, than on subjective ones that would have made him reexamine some of his own hard-and-fast rules.

Whatever the origins of his negativity, Arnold needed to change his teaching style to be more in line with his own goals. Only then would he be able to give the students the lively experience he wanted to, one that would broaden their minds and extend their grasps. If this happened, Arnold could count himself as having succeeded in a challenge he held very dear.

CATCH THE HAPPINESS HABIT

You may call it optimism, happiness, or positive vibes. The way you choose to frame what happens to you—and what you communicate to others— contributes greatly to your quality of life. Psychologists Michael Scheier, PhD, of Carnegie Mellon University in Pittsburgh, and Charles Carver, PhD, of the University of Miami, define optimists as people who expect good things to happen to them, not bad things. Pessimists are just the opposite: They expect to miss out on the good things in life and experience the things that are bad. Being optimistic is the final skill you need to be in control of your life—and it's a fun one, at that!

In reviewing a wide range of studies examining the psychological and physical effects of optimism and pessimism, Dr. Scheier and Dr. Carver reached the following conclusions:

- Optimistic people experience less emotional distress during times of adversity than pessimists.

- When followed over time, optimists experience less distress, while distress levels rise in pessimists.

- Compared with pessimists, optimists report fewer physical symptoms during times of duress and maintain a higher health status during their lives.

- Optimists are less likely to suffer negative side effects from major surgery or to be rehospitalized within the first few months after surgery.

- When diagnosed with a life-threatening illness such as recurrent cancer, people with a less pessimistic outlook outlive those who are more pessimistic.

- Optimists have more efficient immune systems than pessimists.

- Optimists exhibit less extreme surges of blood pressure and heart rate during the course of their daily lives.[1]

In another study, more than 800 cardiac patients were given a battery of tests at the time of their coronary angiograms. Among the tests was one in which the patients were asked to report how strongly they experienced positive emotions: intense joy or ecstasy; bubbles of happiness; being a cheerful, high-spirited person; laughing easily; jumping for joy; being a cheerful optimist; considering themselves especially lighthearted; and using words such as *fantastic* or *sensational* to describe experiences. After these tests were taken, the people were followed for an average of more than 11 years. With all other risk factors but depression taken into account, researchers found significantly lower death rates among those with scores that indicated optimism.[2]

Being positive affects not only your physical health but also your sense of well-being. Take the situation of brothers Harold and Oliver, both in their late eighties. Both are widowers whose children provide cooked meals and other care, so they can continue to live in their own homes. While Oliver tends to focus on the negative, Harold prefers to look on the bright side.

Oliver, 85, still sees and hears adequately. His gait is slow, but he walks without a cane. He had a tumor removed from one shoulder several years ago, and it has not recurred. Other than that, he has no major health problems. He has few visitors.

Harold, 88, is legally blind, although he can make out faces up close. Because of arthritis in his knees, he must wear leg braces to stand up. Voices from the radio and television are his primary companions.

If you stop by to see Oliver, he'll grumble as he walks you into the living room: "I'll tell you, it's not the same in your eighties. My shoulder never has been the same since that tumor. I can't do the things I used to do." When asked about his family, he volunteers a couple of sentences, and then goes back to talking about his shoulder.

On the flip side, if you look in on Harold, chances are you'll hear how wonderful his children are to be so much help. He'll tell you about each of them and talk about his grandchildren. He follows their activities quite closely. His leg braces have made such a difference! He has a great deal to be thankful for. He's delighted by your visit and tells you so.

While the brothers are similar in some ways, Harold is worse off physically, yet he's much happier. Why? He focuses on the positive.

Live the 5-to-1 Ratio

In studies of married couples, University of Washington psychologist John Gottman, PhD, has found that the best predictor of marital longevity is a ratio of five times more positive communications than negative ones.[3] Dr. Gottman is not suggesting that Pollyanna platitudes will save your marriage. Troublesome issues do need to be addressed. You and your partner just need to focus on real problems as opposed to constantly finding fault with each other. Some positives that Dr. Gottman says can ensure a stable relationship include:

- Touching
- Paying compliments
- Smiling
- Sharing joys
- Sharing enthusiasms
- Laughing
- Showing interest and curiosity about what the other partner is experiencing and saying

That's definitely a list of enjoyable things to do, and touching is a good place to start. The value of touch may be rooted in our biology. Decades of research on infants—both human and animal—have shown that touch helps us thrive. When touch-deprived premature babies are given massage therapy, they gain weight faster than similar babies who don't receive massage.[4,5,6] The other positives on the list above make us feel good about ourselves, make life more pleasant, and may even have physical benefits.

On the flip side, you need to be on the lookout for negative actions or reactions, as they can weigh down the ratio and make it harder to achieve that balance. Here's a list of common negatives to avoid.

- Taking critical potshots
- Giving disgusted looks
- Saying "I did not!" or "I am not!"
- Saying "There's a lot wrong with you, too"
- Withdrawing
- Pushing your point of view
- Whining

This list of behaviors represents the dark side of life. There's no question that these habits make other people feel bad. When you're attacked, you're likely to strike back, which can set up an ongoing negative cycle—and none of us wants to live like that! And, as we've seen with aggression, that negative cycle can soon spin out of control.

For the best life possible, try giving yourself and everyone around you five times more positive messages than negative ones. One quick way to do that is to eliminate as many of those negative habits as possible; it's a very efficient way to get that 5-to-1 ratio. In fact, the ratio is almost impossible to achieve without real attention to cutting down on negatives.

This simple 5-to-1 ratio will help you get along better with yourself, your family, your co-workers, and others. And improving those relationships is likely to increase the ratio of positives to negatives in your life as a whole, thus completing your 8-week journey.

Use the 5-to-1 Ratio with Yourself

To be one of life's winners, you need to let yourself know that you already *are* one by adopting an upbeat attitude most of the time. Evidence suggests that such behavior will produce multiple benefits. University of Chicago psychologist Ed Diener, PhD, has shown that when people evaluate their well-being, the ratio of pleasant (positive) to unpleasant (negative) emotions plays a pivotal role over time. This ratio of pleasant to unpleasant emotions arises from how you evaluate events as they happen. Dr. Diener maintains that if you interpret your life as being made up of a string of positive events, you'll experience more pleasant than unpleasant emotions over time—so adopting an upbeat perspective is a key factor in your sense of overall well-being.[7]

Let's listen to Sasha's self-talk one typical Wednesday evening.

- "I'm going to be a dud on the committee looking into new computers. I don't know all that much."

- "My nose is crooked."

- "Mary probably won't like the present I got her. I'm no good at choosing presents."

- "Pearl's microwave is nicer than mine. Some people have all the luck. I wish I were lucky. I'm unlucky, actually."

Instead of punishing herself with this steady litany of negative messages, she might have observed:

- "I'm the only person on the committee who sits at a work station all day. They're fortunate to have my perspective."

- "My eyes are quite attractive."

- "Mary should be pleased I'm giving her a present. I'm good about remembering birthdays."

- "I'm fortunate to own a microwave. It makes cooking so much easier!"

Both sets of observations are true in a sense—but what a difference in perspective!

British psychiatrist Michael Rutter, MD, notes that a person's resilience and ability to bounce back from adversity are determined by the ability to act positively in such situations. This ability comes not only from how you feel about yourself but also from the problem-solving skills you've learned.[8] In other words, your disposition isn't fixed at birth or in childhood. You now know how to solve some problems. You may have been mopey as a child, but learning to be positive now will let you reap great advantages. Positive emotions have been linked to everything from fewer colds to improved resistance to HIV/AIDS.

List your five best traits. Think of positive characteristics about yourself that you could add to your self-talk on a regular basis. What do you think are your strengths? What do others say about you that could be interpreted as praise?

- Are you a good listener?

- Can you be enthusiastic?

- Can you be helpful?

- What's your best physical feature?

- Are there areas in which you try hard?

- Do you ever make someone else's life better?

Keep thinking until you come up with a list of at least five of your good features, and then write them in your notebook. Next, take as long as you need to memorize your list. Alternatively, you could list the items on small cards or pieces of paper to put on your mirror and in your shirt pocket. From now on, every time you catch yourself engaging in negative self-talk, stop! Recall or look at your list of positives and repeat it to yourself before you say another negative word.

Pledge to stop your five worst self-talk messages. Another essential part of Week 8 is to reduce the overall number of negative messages you give yourself. Yes, sometimes everyone has to be a little bit self-critical. But you need to be sure that your self-criticisms address only those specific situations in which it's important that you change your behavior or correct an outside problem. Let all the others go! Think of five unnecessary negative things you routinely say about yourself and write them in your notebook. Next, draw a big circle around them and put a thick slash through it as a visual reminder—no more trash talk allowed!

Count five of your blessings. All of us have much to be grateful for, including the precious gift of life, so come up with five positive aspects of your world. You probably have one or more people who love you. Maybe you have an exciting vocation or avocation, or your mind has been liberated by your education. Perhaps you're grateful for the solace you receive from religion or some other spiritual activity. Most likely you're free from serious want. Ponder your blessings, and then write at least five of them in your notebook.

Pledge to stop complaints about the world. It's equally important to limit calling attention to the flip sides of these blessings. Negative self-talk about your world should make you pause and ask yourself, "What exactly am I grousing about?"

With the topic clearly in mind, ask the four I AM WORTH IT questions.

1. Is what I'm complaining about Important to me?

2. Is my reaction Appropriate?

3. Can I Modify this situation? (If not, go back and review five of your blessings.)

4. Would it be **WORTH IT** to try? (If not, review five of your blessings with self-talk.)

If you answer all four questions with a yes, apply problem solving, assertion, or saying no to try to get this situation changed so you can turn it from a negative into a positive. If that's expecting too much, try at least for some movement in a positive direction.

Some topics we habitually complain about (to ourselves and others) are really gratuitous. We need to remember how toxic negative energy can be, not only to the soul but also to the body. In your notebook, list five things that you can stop complaining about. Each time you catch yourself about to repeat this old counterproductive behavior, distract yourself by refocusing your attention.

Use the 5-to-1 Ratio with Your Partner

Sasha has been married for 20 years. At first, she and Josef exchanged a lot of positives. Now she's more likely to say things like:

- "You may have washed the car, but there's still dirt on the tires. You never remember the tires."
- "You never want to go anywhere."
- "I think your hairline has receded further."
- (Without first listening to Josef) "Let me tell you about my day!"

How would the relationship change if she reported equally accurate information from the following perspective instead?

- "Thanks for washing the car. It looks much better."
- "I'd love for us to plan a date."
- "Your eyes have always been a turn-on for me. They still are."
- "Honey, what was your day like?"

Dr. Gottman's research on couples suggests that if Sasha spoke the second way, she would have more cooperation and attention from her husband and more good times with him. She also would have a more positive attitude about her lot in life.

Count the ways you love him (or her). If you have a partner, focus on that person. If not, focus on your closest relationship. What do you admire about him? What first attracted you? What are some qualities your friends admire? Can you think of ways in which he is usually kind? What are his most attractive physical features? In your notebook, write down five things you love and respect about this person. Also record a recent incident in which he really helped you; think of a way you can let him know how much that meant to you. Best of all, notice when your significant other behaves well, share this observation immediately, and express appreciation for what you've just observed.

Clarify your negatives selectively. When it comes to negatives, the goal is not to eliminate all criticism. Instead, when you have to tell your partner you're unhappy with something, your comments should refer to a specific problem that needs addressing, with the larger goal of improving the relationship. You need to be selective so the criticism isn't overwhelming. Also, if you need to criticize your partner to keep the relationship good, grant reciprocity. What is it about you that your partner thinks really needs to change? (As you learned in Week 6, you're not truly listening unless you're prepared to be changed by what you hear!)

In truth, most negative interactions don't improve a relationship, even if that's the goal of the "suggestions." As we observed about listening, advice is easily perceived as veiled criticism. Think of which of these behaviors you are ready to let go of.

This leaves the criticisms that are necessary. Write down this initial list in your notebook. Try to be as specific as possible. For instance: "I will stop being so critical of Roger's ideas for saving money" is more specific than "I will stop being so critical of Roger." Next, test each entry with the I AM WORTH IT questions. What would be the best way to approach the other person? Brainstorm ways you can deal with it so the criticism doesn't harm your relationship. Then wait. You'll need to repeat the exercise only if a similar situation arises and you get four new yes answers to the I AM WORTH IT questions. Wait for an upsetting situation and address that specific occasion only when you practice assertion.

Use the 5-to-1 Ratio with Young Children

One of the most essential times to practice the 5-to-1 ratio is when you're dealing with children. Educational researchers report that young children who hear *a lot more positives than negatives* from birth through age 3 grow up to have higher verbal intelligence.[9] (Of course, parents should also insist that children shape up when they behave badly.[10])

To become successful adults, your children need both honest praise and insistence on good behavior, but you need to give a lot more praise than criticism. It's also important to be interested in and respectful of your children as real people. Young children get a lot of their first view of the world from the adults around them.

Create positive moments through reinforcement. When you listen to your child, you let him know that he has important things to say. Often, it's good to repeat what you've just heard, then add a sentence or two that reinforces the child for having said something worth hearing: "So the score was tied, you were running down the field kicking the ball as you ran, and this big guy was coming at you from the other direction. You must feel really good that you were able to pass the ball off to Ron before that other guy got all the way down the field."

With younger children, your reinforcement may be occasioned by the child's action rather than something that was said: "Carole, I see you have the ball. Can you tell me what color it is?"

When you give your child attention, you let him know he is worth spending time with. When he's learning to play a musical instrument and you take the time to listen to him perform, you're sending the message that he is capable of entertaining others. When you play a game with a child, you send the message that engaging in an activity with him is worth your time. When you include children in your own activities, you let them know they're positive additions to the scene.

List five ways in which you can affect your child's worldview with positive reinforcement.

Frame discipline in a positive way. Children need to be held to standards of behavior, with expectations that they can conform to those standards. You also need to be lavish with your praise. What is the child good at? What has she done recently that's noteworthy? Can you catch her being helpful? Reinforce good behavior whenever you can. Be honest, though— false praise devalues everything else you say as well. Think of five ways you can reframe your negative discipline into positive reinforcement, and write it down in your notebook.

Listening, attention, and praise all tell a child that she is valued. Such lucky children are likely to grow up with high self-esteem. Are there any young children in your life? If so, get to work on helping them grow up with high self-esteem.

Use the 5-to-1 Ratio with Teens

If you have relationships with children in their teens, they probably don't praise you very often. Teenagers are at the stage in life when they begin to break away from being children, especially in their family. They're growing up, which can be very hard to do, so they are probably trying to make it easier to break away by focusing on the negative: "*Sarah's* mother fixes a wonderful hot meal every night. *She* cares about her kids."

Try not to react in kind: "Well, if your room and the living room weren't so messy, maybe I'd have more time to cook." Instead, at most, you might want to reply, "It sounds like Sarah's mother is a good cook and cares about her kids. Well, I care about you, too!" Silence is probably an even better option.

If you are patient, your teen will outgrow this chronic focus on the negative. The knee-jerk impulse to criticize you is a stage. Meanwhile, no matter how hard it is, try to keep a positive focus. Remember how insecure you felt as a teen? Chances are, your teenager feels the same way!

Be available to listen by spending time with your teen. Occasionally, he may decide to reveal something close to his heart.

Limit your criticism to things that really matter. Focus your criticisms on a few selective matters of greatest importance to you. You're much more likely to be heard. Is it being on time? Doing homework? Mowing the lawn? Keeping the bedroom neat? Being respectful? Contributing to family finances? Driving safely? Not smoking? Choosing your battles wisely will make you a more effective and fair parent.

Be loud and proud with your praise. Let your teen know some of the things you really like.

- "It's great the way you help your brother understand his math homework."

- "I appreciate your listening to my point of view."

- "You are always so kind to your grandmother."

- "When you kicked the ball so straight, it really put your teammates in scoring range."

Use the 5-to-1 Ratio with Your Parents

It's time to face facts: If your parents are older, they probably have a limited number of years left. Another fact: If they have been whiners for their entire lives, they're not likely to change now. (They may have even more aches and pains than before.) Also, if they have always been overbearing, losing a sense of power over their own lives will probably make them more heavy-handed.

Stay in control of the negatives. You can protect yourself from being manipulated by your parents by simply being aware of negative thoughts and feelings. You'll need to ask the I AM WORTH IT questions. Deflect, solve problems, and assert yourself as needed. List five of the negative patterns you have with your parents and brainstorm a strategy for stopping each.

In a related matter, sometimes we let long-ago battles with our parents influence the way we treat everyone now. If your father always told you what to do, maybe you're determined that now, no one is *ever* going to do that again—and there you are, always stuck in an oppositional stance. Or perhaps your mother insisted that your room be neat, and now your home couldn't pass a health inspection.

While the parent in question may no longer be living, and you may feel as though you're making choices about your behavior free and clear of that influence, reconsider the matter. Behaving in exact opposition to those past messages would mean that your parent is still determining your behavior, albeit now in a 180-degree fashion. If this is the case, you still aren't free — and you're probably sabotaging yourself in the process.

Another negative pattern is to internalize parental criticism. You may tell yourself that you're lazy or incompetent or not pretty enough. These messages are probably untrue, or at least they can become untrue if you deliberately choose to behave differently. Send yourself your own messages, and make them positive.

True liberation will come when you can see each situation for what it is and then behave thoughtfully, in a manner appropriate to that circumstance and that circumstance only. That's being in real control.

Let compassion be your positive motivation. At the same time you are protecting yourself, be compassionate with your parents. Their world is slowly but surely shrinking. They probably would really like you to view them favorably. One way to ensure that they feel honored and know how much you love them is to give them five positives for each negative. Write down five positives for each living parent in your notebook and make a point of adding more in your contact with them.

Use the 5-to-1 Ratio at Work

Ever since the publication of Dr. Daniel Goleman's popular *Emotional Intelligence* books in 1995 and 1997, businesses the world over have become interested in increasing the emotional intelligence of their workforce.[11] Their motivation is to increase profits. Studies show that workers who are not depressed are more productive and absent less often.[12]

Another study showed that workers who are not hostile tend to return to work sooner after being ill. Interviews with 2 million employees at 700 American companies found that the greatest determining factor in how long an employee will stay at one job — and how productive he is — is the quality of the working relationship with an immediate boss.[13] And the leading organization for training top managers, the Center for Creative Leadership, reports that workers who succeed in top leadership positions tend to be flexible, have good relationships, control their own behavior, are open to constructive criticism and opportunities to learn, and possess good social skills.

We would argue that the quality of being positive is intrinsic to all these characteristics of successful leadership. If you're a supervisor, you need to tell the people you supervise when they do something wrong or simply how they could perform better, especially if changes were made in the way they approach a particular task. On the other hand, your employees need to enjoy their work, and the key to that is feeling that they're doing a good job and that their work is appreciated. Thus, both kinds of feedback, the positive and the critical, are essential. Be sure that the amount of positive feedback far outweighs the negative. Also, be sure that your employees understand why you're excited about the goals and objectives of the enterprise. You need to project a positive attitude toward the company and your own work.

These same guidelines can apply to your interactions with your peers and even your own supervisor. Here are a few ways you can use the 5-to-1 ratio at work.

Improve the ratio of positives to negatives with your employees. You write the annual reviews of the people you supervise. This piece of paper affects their likelihood of raises, future promotions, and even keeping their jobs. They deserve ongoing feedback, not just an annual review that may seem to them to come out of left field. Each week, try to let your employees know in what ways they're performing well. They should be told what areas need improvement and what specific suggestions you have for better performance. Remember to aim for five positives for each negative.

Another positive interaction with employees is listening while they tell you what's right and wrong about your organization. At least a few times during the week, try to have an open-door policy or regularly scheduled one-on-one meetings.

Improve the ratio of positives to negatives with peer colleagues. Globalization has resulted in people of many cultures working together, often from different locations. This means that you need to familiarize yourself with the cultures of all your work colleagues before you can even know what qualifies as positive or negative.

Even if all your colleagues have backgrounds similar to yours, you're still faced with a newly urgent need to understand each other. The rapid rate of technological change has resulted in projects so complex that large teams must work together to make a product operational. In many companies, the old hierarchical arrangement of power has given way to brainstorming and joint decision making. This requires a level of cooperation beyond that needed in the past. Try to brainstorm five specific ways you can improve your peer relationships, and write them down in your notebook.

Improve the ratio of positives to negatives with your supervisor. One of your supervisor's responsibilities is to have a good working relationship with you, so both of you are invested in that goal. As with your co-workers, you can succeed in having a good relationship with your boss by applying what you've already learned. When something at your workplace bothers you, first clarify exactly what it is. The I AM WORTH IT questions will help you decide whether to try to change your reaction or the situation. If it's the latter, and your supervisor is the problem, *ask for an appointment* and then practice assertion. If it's a problem that needs solving, bring it to the supervisor's attention and suggest a brainstorming session with everyone involved.

Often, you may be in a position where you can't say no to your boss. Instead, ask for help. The other skills to focus on with your supervisor are speaking up and listening and empathy. Think of five ways you can use these skills to improve the positive ratio of your relationship, and write them down in your notebook.

ARNOLD LEARNS TO FOCUS ON THE POSITIVE

At Highland Park High School, one of the responsibilities of the department heads was to occasionally sit in on classes taught by members of the department. Afterward, the chairman would provide feedback, with the goal of helping the teacher improve. About 4 weeks into the fall semester, the English department chairman, Charles, visited Arnold's class. Unknown to Arnold, several students had complained to the guidance department about his teaching. Charles made Arnold a little more nervous than usual by taking notes throughout the class.

After school that day, Charles came by. "You seem to have a great grasp of Tennyson," he said. He also complimented Arnold's references to outside works of criticism. "The intellectual rigor needed in the honors section was evident throughout the class. Students need to develop clarity of thought, and you are clearly helping them to do that.

"Tell me, Arnold," Charles continued, "do you like the early poems of Tennyson?"

"Yes. I admire the concept of love as the supreme experience and reality of life," Arnold replied. Then he was struck by a memory of his own high school English teacher, which he shared with Charles. Mr. Smith, his teacher, had told Arnold that he appeared to understand Tennyson's appreciation of the importance of feelings. This had led Arnold to write a poem about his own adolescent feeling of disgust with society, which, with Arnold's permission, Mr. Smith had read to the class.

Charles said, "This high school class seems to have really affected you."

"Yes. Maybe it's even part of why I ended up majoring in English literature," Arnold said. He remembered that it was in Mr. Smith's class that he began to get an insight into the beauty and the intricacies of literature. The teacher encouraged his most sterling insights and praised him for them. This had led Arnold to do something extra, and Mr. Smith had rewarded that, too.

Arnold suddenly realized that a pattern had been repeated throughout the school year: Mr. Smith had marked every misspelling and every grammar mistake, sometimes even suggesting alternative wording—but the main point had always been what was best about Arnold's work.

Charles ended their meeting by asking Arnold if he could remember what the most influential aspect of Mr. Smith's teaching had been. Arnold said he would have to think about it. When he did, he realized that it was his former teacher's positive focus.

For the rest of the week, Arnold took a tape recorder to the honors class. This spooked the students even more, but it did provide Arnold with some useful information. Listening to the tapes, he realized that he spent as much time attacking students' comments as he did encouraging further development of what they said. The more critical he was, the less likely the student was to continue speaking.

Changing his approach wasn't easy. Arnold didn't want to sacrifice intellectual rigor. A Pollyanna-ish, "everything you say is beautiful" approach would be distasteful. How could he keep the class rigorous yet add a positive thrust? Arnold spent all weekend toiling over his lesson plans for the coming week.

On Monday, Arnold announced an end to the grading rule that more than two style or grammar mistakes would equal at most a C. The week went a little better. When he recorded the class again that Friday, he found that the ratio was closer to two positives to one negative.

This process continued for a month. By spring, most students passed the advanced-placement exam in English literature and composition. Despite the fact that this credit exempted many of them from a lit class in college, nearly every student eventually took at least one.

Arnold's new method of encouragement carried over to the rest of his classes. Two years later, the yearbook was dedicated to him.

Week 8 Recap

In your relationships, aim for five positive interactions for each negative one when dealing with:

- Yourself
- Your partner
- Your young children
- Your teens
- Your parents
- Your work associates

EPILOGUE: WELCOME TO LIFE MORE UNDER YOUR CONTROL

Now that you've completed the 8 weeks, turn to the Appendix to retake the Self-Assessment Quiz. When you compare your new score with your initial test results to see where you are and how far you've come, you'll probably see that your scores have improved. (Try again in six months to see if you've made more progress.)

When you think about your life, especially situations that used to rankle you or send you running for cover, are you more aware early on of all your thoughts and feelings? Before you act, do you take the time to evaluate whatever situation is evoking negative reactions? When you decide to just live with the situation, can you find ways to calm yourself down—and do you succeed at it more often than you did before?

You now have effective skills that can help you solve problems, get others to behave differently, and stay in control of your time, money, and good name. When you decide to act, are you using these skills and behaving in ways that are in line with your best interest?

You're no doubt seeing improvements in your relationships as well. Do you understand how to make yourself heard? When you listen, do you *really* listen? Do you find yourself understanding people's motives, and does this understanding help you devise better solutions to conflicts?

Most important, are you happier? Are you better able to see the beauty in the world, the positive spin that can give color and light to all your life? Do you let this improvement in your mood and your outlook spill over into all of your relationships?

If so, we've done our job. Your new coping skills will stay with you for life, helping you to handle whatever comes along. As a consequence, you will begin to positively affect the environment around you. Like a pebble tossed into the water, your actions will have a ripple effect throughout your world. And you just may end up moving mountains.

THE SELF-ASSESSMENT QUIZ

NEVER		SOMETIMES		ALWAYS

1. I know right away when I'm angry.

1	2	3	4	5

2. If it's bad weather on my day off, I get over it quickly.

1	2	3	4	5

3. My stress level is low.

1	2	3	4	5

4. If stuck without a ride, I find a way of getting where I want to go.

1	2	3	4	5

5. When the waiter brings the wrong dish, I ask for a replacement.

1	2	3	4	5

6. I'm good at saying no.

1	2	3	4	5

7. I can tell people what I'm feeling.

1	2	3	4	5

8. In conversations, I listen about half the time.

1	2	3	4	5

9. On airplanes, parents of crying toddlers don't bother me.

1	2	3	4	5

NEVER	SOMETIMES	ALWAYS

10. I look for things to praise in others.

1   2   3   4   5

11. I know right away when I'm sad.

1   2   3   4   5

12. Traffic jams don't bother me for very long.

1   2   3   4   5

13. In a close game, I quickly get over an unfair call by the referee.

1   2   3   4   5

14. When I have a problem, I ask others for ideas.

1   2   3   4   5

15. I ask for a change when the car radio is tuned to a station I don't like.

1   2   3   4   5

16. I keep the number of tasks I take on to a manageable level.

1   2   3   4   5

17. In disagreements, I focus on specific situations, not general trends.

1   2   3   4   5

18. I avoid giving advice unless asked.

1   2   3   4   5

19. I'm okay with people with driving styles different from mine.

1   2   3   4   5

20. Most of my close relationships go well.

1   2   3   4   5

21. I'm aware of my feelings.

1   2   3   4   5

22. In bad situations, I can be counted on to be effective.

1   2   3   4   5

23. When returning home after a tough day, I put it aside.

1   2   3   4   5

NEVER   SOMETIMES   ALWAYS

24. I'm good at problem solving.

   1   2   3   4   5

25. When interrupted, I manage to continue speaking.

   1   2   3   4   5

26. My rewards at work are fair.

   1   2   3   4   5

27. I hold up my side of a conversation.

   1   2   3   4   5

28. In disagreements, I realize I could be wrong.

   1   2   3   4   5

29. I can accept as okay people with politics different from mine.

   1   2   3   4   5

30. When my significant other mispronounces a word, I say nothing.

   1   2   3   4   5

CALCULATING YOUR SCORE

Now that you've taken the quiz, you can determine your profile on the 10 skills that help you stay in control. Copy the numbers you circled for each question into your notebook, then refer to the notebook as you fill in the section below. To evaluate your score, turn back to page 39.

Awareness

How aware are you of your feelings? (Skill 1)

    I.   _____

    II.   _____

    21.   _____

    Total _____

Evaluation

How often do you think situations through before reacting? (Skill 2)

2. _____

12. _____

22. _____

Total _____

Deflection

Can you get over negative thoughts and/or feelings you don't want to have? (Skill 3)

3. _____

13. _____

23. _____

Total _____

Solving problems

Are you good at solving problems? (Skill 4)

4. _____

14. _____

24. _____

Total _____

Standing up for yourself

Do you ask for what you need and want? (Skill 5)

5. _____

15. _____

25. _____

Total _____

Are you self-protective? (Skill 6)

6. _____

16. _____

26. _____

Total _____

Communicating effectively

Do you speak in ways that make others likely to listen? (Skill 7)

7. _____

17. _____

27. _____

· Total _____

Do you listen effectively? (Skill 8)

8. _____

18. _____

28. _____

Total _____

Understanding others

Do you understand others? (Skill 9)

9. _____

19. _____

29. _____

Total _____

Embodying positive values

Is your emphasis positive? (Skill 10)

10. _____

20. _____

30. _____

Total _____

Total
score: _____ (sum of all scores)

NOTES

CHAPTER 1. THE SCIENTIFIC PERSPECTIVE

1. R. B. Williams et al., "Type A Behavior, Hostility, and Coronary Atherosclerosis," *Psychosomatic Medicine* 42 (1980): 539–49.

2. J. C. Barefoot, W. G. Dahlstrom, and R. B. Williams, "Hostility, CHD Incidence, and Total Mortality: A 25-Year Follow-Up Study of 255 Physicians," *Psychosomatic Medicine* 45 (1983): 59–63.

3. R. B. Williams, "A 69-Year-Old Man with Anger and Angina," *Journal of the American Medical Association* 282 (1999): 763–70.

4. Findings presented at the 2000 annual meeting of the Society of Behavioral Medicine; manuscript currently under journal review.

5. J. C. Barefoot and M. Schroll, "Symptoms of Depression, Acute Myocardial Infarction, and Total Mortality in a Community Sample," *Circulation* 93 (1996): 1976–80; N. Frasure-Smith, F. Lesperance, and M. Talajic, "Depression Following Myocardial Infarction: Impact on 6-Month Survival," *Journal of the American Medical Association* 270 (1993): 1819–25.

6. G. Hawthorne et al., "The Excess Cost of Depression in South Australia: A Population Study," *Australian and New Zealand Journal of Psychiatry* 37 (2003): 362–73; H. G. Birnbaum, S. A. Leong, and P. E. Greenberg, "The Economics of Women and Depression: An Employer's Perspective," *Journal of Affective Disorders* 74 (2003): 15–22.

7. J. S. House, K. R. Landis, and D. Umberson, "Social Relationships and Health," *Science* 241 (1988): 540–45.

8. R. A. Karasek and T. Theorell, *Healthy Work: Stress, Productivity, and the Reconstruction of Working Life* (New York: Basic Books, 1992).

9. I. C. Siegler et al., "Hostility during Late Adolescence Predicts Coronary Risk Factors at Midlife," *American Journal of Epidemiology* 136 (1992): 146–54.

10. R. B. Williams et al., "Psychosocial Correlates of Job Strain in a Sample of Working Women," *Archives of General Psychiatry* 54 (1997): 543–48.

11. R. B. Williams, "Neurobiology, Cellular and Molecular Biology, and Psychosomatic Medicine," *Psychosomatic Medicine* 56 (1994): 308–15.

12. R. B. Williams, J. C. Barefoot, and N. Schneiderman, "Psychosocial Risk Factors in Cardiovascular Disease: More Than One Culprit at Work." *JAMA* 209 (October 22, 2003): 1–4.

13. Williams, "Neurobiology," 308–15; S. B. Manuck, M. E. Bleil, K. L. Petersen, J. D. Flory, J. J. Mann, R. E. Ferrell, and M. F. Muldoon, "The Socio-economic Status of Communities Predicts Variation in Brain Serotonergic Responsivity," *Psychological Medicine* 35, no. 4 (April 2005): 519–28; F. A. Matthews, J. D. Flory, M. F. Muldoon, and S. B. Manuck, "Does Socioeconomic Status Relate to Central Serotonergic Responsivity in Healthy Adults?" *Psychosomatic Medicine* 62, no. 2 (March–April 2000): 231–37.

14. K. P. Lesch et al., "Association of Anxiety-Related Traits with a Polymorphism in the Serotonin Transporter Gene Regulatory Region," *Science* 274 (1996): 1527–31; R. B. Williams et al., "Central Nervous System Serotonin Function and Cardiovascular Responses to Stress," *Psychosomatic Medicine* 63 (2001): 300–305.

15. N. Frasure-Smith, F. Lesperance, and M. Talajic, "Depression Following Myocardial Infarction: Impact on 6-Month Survival," *Journal of the American Medical Association* 270 (1993): 1819–25.

16. R. B. Williams et al., "Prognostic Importance of Social and Economic Resources among Medically Treated Patients with Angiographically Documented Coronary Artery Disease," *Journal of the American Medical Association* 267 (1992): 520–24.

17. M. E. P. Seligman, *Learned Optimism* (New York: Knopf, 1991).

18. M. F. Scheier et al., "Optimism and Rehospitalization after Coronary Artery Bypass Graft Surgery," *Archives of Internal Medicine* 159 (1999): 829–35.

19. S. Strack, C. S. Carver, and P. H. Blaney, "Predicting Successful Completion of an Aftercare Program Following Treatment for Alcoholism: The Role of Dispositional Optimism," *Journal of Personality and Social Psychology* 53 (1987): 579–84.

20. I. Brissette, M. F. Scheier, and C. S. Carver, "The Role of Optimism in Social Network Development, Coping, and Psychological Adjustment during a Life Transition," *Journal of Personality and Social Psychology* 82 (2002): 102–11.

21. T. Maruta et al., "Optimists vs. Pessimists: Survival Rate among Medical Patients Over a 30-Year Period," *Mayo Clinic Proceedings* 75 (2000): 140–43.

22. B. L. Fredrickson and R. W. Levenson, "Positive Emotions Speed Recovery from the Cardiovascular Sequelae of Negative Emotions," *Cognition and Emotion* 12 (1998): 191–220.

23. T. W. Kamarck, B. Annunziato, and L. M. Amateau, "Affiliation Moderates the Effects of Social Threat on Stress-Related Cardiovascular Responses: Boundary Conditions for a Laboratory Model of Social Support," *Psychosomatic Medicine* 57 (1995): 183–94.

24. P. Salovey and J. Mayer, "What Is Emotional Intelligence?" in *Emotional Development and Emotional Intelligence: Implications for Educators,* eds. P. Salovey and D. Sluyter (New York: Basic Books, 1997).

25. D. Goleman, *Emotional Intelligence: Why It Can Matter More Than IQ* (New York: Bantam, 1995) and *Working with Emotional Intelligence* (New York: Bantam, 1998).

26. M. Csikszentmihalyi, *Optimal Experience: Psychological Studies of Flow in Consciousness* (Cambridge, England: Cambridge University Press, 1988).

27. A. Bandura, "Self-Efficacy: Toward a Unifying Theory of Behavioral Change," *Psychological Review* 84 (1977): 191–215.

28. M. Rutter, H. Giller, and A. Hagell, *Antisocial Behavior by Young People* (Cambridge, England: Cambridge University Press, 1998).

29. L. J. Luecken, "Attachment and Loss Experiences during Childhood Are Associated with Adult Hostility, Depression, and Social Support," *Journal of Psychosomatic Research* 49 (2000): 85–91.

30. ——, "Childhood Attachment and Loss Experiences Affect Adult Cardiovascular and Cortisol Function," *Psychosomatic Medicine* 60 (1998): 765–72.

31. Amy J. Kraft and Linda Luecken, "Cortisol Stress Response in Adult Children of Divorce Is Related to Perceptions of Parental Caring," *Annals of Behavioral Medicine* 29 (2005 Supplement, poster at April meeting): 141.

32. I. Lissau-Lund-Sorensen and T. I. A. Sorensen, "Prospective Study of the Influence of Social Factors in Childhood on the Risk of Overweight in Young Adulthood," *International Journal of Obesity* 16 (1992): 169–75; "Parental Neglect during Childhood and Increased Risk of Obesity in Young Adulthood," *Lancet* 343 (1994): 324–27.

33. E. Hart and T. R. Risley, *Meaningful Differences in the Everyday Experience of Young American Children* (Baltimore: Paul H. Brookes, 1995).

34. K. L. Matthews et al., "Negative Family Environment as a Predictor of Boys' Future Status on Measures of Hostile Attitudes, Interview Behavior, and Anger Expression," *Health Psychology* 14 (1996): 30–37.

35. J. Kagan, "The Role of Parents in Children's Psychological Development," *Pediatrics* 104 (1999): 164–67.

36. A. Caspi et al., "Role of Genotype in the Cycle of Violence in Maltreated Children," *Science* 297 (2002): 851–54.

37. F. I. Fawzy et al., "Malignant Melanoma: Effects of an Early Structured Psychiatric Intervention, Coping, and Affective State on Recurrence and Survival 6 Years Later," *Archives of General Psychiatry* 50 (1993): 681–89.

38. M. Friedman, C. E. Thoresen, and J. J. Gill, "Alteration of Type A Behavior and Its Effect on Cardiac Recurrences in Post Myocardial Infarction Patients: Summary Results of the Recurrent Coronary Prevention Project," *American Heart Journal* 112 (1986): 653–65.

39. J. A. Blumenthal et al., "Stress Management and Exercise Training in Cardiac Patients with Myocardial Ischemia," *Archives of Internal Medicine* 157 (1997): 2213–23.

40. Y. Gidron, K. Davidson, and I. Bata, "The Short-Term Effects of a Hostility-Reduction Intervention in CHD Patients," *Health Psychology* 18 (1999): 416–20.

41. G. D. Bishop et al., "Effects of a Psychosocial Skills Training Workshop on Psychophysiological and Psychosocial Risk in Patients Undergoing Coronary Artery Bypass Grafting," *American Heart Journal* 150 (2005): 602–9.

CHAPTER 2. ARE YOU IN CONTROL?

1. M. C. Hocking et al., "Development of a New LifeSkills Scale to Measure a 'Positive' Psychosocial Risk Factor Profile." Poster session presented at the annual meeting of the Society for Behavioral Medicine (March 2003), Salt Lake City, Utah.

CHAPTER 3. WEEK 1: RECOGNIZE YOUR EMOTIONS

1. S. Nicolaidis, ed. *Serotonergic System, Feeding and Body Weight Regulation* (New York: Academic Press, 1986).

2. Paul Ekman and Walter V. Friesen, *Unmasking the Face: A Guide to Reading Emotions from Facial Clues* (Englewood Cliffs, N.J.: Prentice-Hall, 1975); Paul Ekman, "Facial Expression and Emotion: 1992 Award Address," *American Psychologist* 48 (April 1993): 384–92.

CHAPTER 4. WEEK 2: WEIGH THE EVIDENCE

1. J. C. Barefoot, W. G. Dahlstrom, and R. B. Williams, "Hostility, CHD Incidence, and Total Mortality: A 25-Year Follow-up Study of 255 Physicians," *Psychosomatic Medicine* 45 (1983): 59–63.

CHAPTER 5. WEEK 3: GAIN CONTROL OF YOUR REACTIONS

1. J. S. Beck, *Cognitive Therapy: Basics and Beyond* (New York: Guilford Press, 1995).

2. D. S. Sobel and R. Ornstein, *The Healthy Mind, Healthy Body Handbook* (Los Altos, Calif.: DRx, 1996), 150, 162, 175; Phillip W. Long, www.mentalhealth.com.

3. J. W. Lehman and H. Benson, "Nonpharmacologic Treatment of Hypertension: A Review," *General Hospital Psychiatry* 4, no. 1 (April 1982): 27–32.

4. R. H. Schneider et al., "Behavioral Treatment of Hypertensive Heart Disease in African-Americans: Rationale and Design of a Randomized Controlled Trial," *Behavioral Medicine* 27: 83–95; R. H. Schneider et al., "Long-Term Effects of Stress Reduction on Mortality in Persons ≥ 55 Years of Age with Systemic Hypertension," *American Journal of Cardiology* 95 (2005): 1060–64

5. P. Carrington, "Modern Forms of Meditation," in P. M. Lehrer and R. L. Woolfolk, eds., *Principles and Practice of Stress Management* (New York: Guilford Press, 1993), 139–41.

CHAPTER 6. WEEK 4: RESOLVE PROBLEMS AND IMPLEMENT SOLUTIONS

1. Society for Human Resource Management, "Work-Life Balance," *Workplace Visions* 4 (2002): 2.

CHAPTER 7. WEEK 5: ASSERT YOURSELF AND LEARN TO SAY NO

1. Annette Peters et al., "Exposure to Traffic and the Onset of Myocardial Infarction, *The New England Journal of Medicine* 21, no. 351 (October 2004): 1721–30.

2. National Highway Traffic Safety Administration and American Automobile Association, www.nhtsa.dot.gov/people/injur/aggressive/aggproplanner/page05/htm.

3. *Business Week,* March 22, 1999: 94E.

4. B. J. Bushman, R. F. Baumeister, and A. D. Stack, "Catharsis, Aggression, and Persuasive Influence: Self-Fulfilling or Self-Defeating Prophecies?" *Journal of Personality and Social Psychology* 76 (January 1999): 367–76.

5. Shelley Taylor, *The Tending Instinct: How Nurturing Is Essential to Who We Are and How We Live* (New York: Times Books, 2002).

6. B. R. Sarason, G. R. Pierce, and I. G. Sarason, *Social Support: An Interactional View* (New York: John Wiley, 1990).

7. Society for Human Resource Management Research, *Workplace Visions* 4 (2002): 2–8.

CHAPTER 10. WEEK 8: LEARN TO LOOK UP

1. M. F. Scheier and C. S. Carver, "Optimism," in G. Fink, ed., *Encyclopedia of Stress* (New York: Academic Press, 2000), 99–102.

2. B. H. Brummett et al., "Ratings of Positive and Depressive Emotion as Predictors of Mortality in Coronary Patients," *International Journal of Cardiology* 100, no. 2 (April 20, 2005): 213-16.

3. J. M. Gottman, *Why Marriages Succeed or Fail: What You Can Learn from the Breakthrough Research to Make Your Marriage Last* (New York: Simon & Schuster, 1994); *What Predicts Divorce? The Relationship between Marital Processes and Marital Outcome* (Hillside, N.Y.: Lawrence Erlbaum, 1994).

4. C. M. Kuhn and S. M. Schanberg, "Responses to Maternal Separation: Mechanisms and Mediators," *International Journal of Developmental Neuroscience* 16 (June/July 1998): 261–70.

5. F. A. Scafidi, T. Field, and S. M. Schanberg, "Factors That Predict Which Preterm Infants Benefit Most from Massage Therapy," *Journal of Developmental and Behavioral Pediatrics* 14 (June 1993): 176–80.

6. C. M. Kuhn et al., "Tactile-Kinesthetic Stimulation Effects on Sympathetic and Adreno-cortical Function in Preterm Infants," *Journal of Pediatrics* 119 (September 1991): 434–40.

7. E. Diener and R. J. Larsen, "The Experience of Emotional Well-Being," in M. Lewis and J. Haviland, eds., *Handbook of Emotions* (New York: Guilford Press, 1993), 405–15.

8. M. Rutter. "Resilience in the Face of Adversity: Protective Factors and Resistance to Psychiatric Disorder," *British Journal of Psychiatry* 147 (December 1985): 598–611.

9. B. Hart and T. R. Risley, *Meaningful Differences in the Everyday Experience of Young American Children* (Baltimore: Paul H. Brookes, 1995).

10. W. Damon, *Greater Expectations: Overcoming the Culture of Indulgence in America's Homes and Schools* (New York: Free Press, 1995).

11. D. Goleman. *Emotional Intelligence: Why It Can Matter More Than IQ* (New York: Bantam, 1995); *Working with Emotional Intelligence* (New York: Bantam, 1998); D. Goleman, R. Boyatzis, and A. McKee, *Primal Leadership: Realizing the Power of Emotional Intelligence* (Boston: Harvard Business School Press, 2002).

12. B. G. Druss, M. Schlesinger, and H. M. Allen, "Depressive Symptoms, Satisfaction with Health Care, and 2-Year Work Outcomes in an Employed Population," *American Journal of Psychiatry* 158 (2001): 731–34.

13. A. Zipkin, "The Wisdom of Thoughtfulness," quoted in Daniel Goleman et al., *Primal Leadership: Realizing the Power of Emotional Intelligence* (Boston: Harvard Business School Press, 2002), 83.

INDEX

Boldface page references indicate charts.
Underscored references indicate boxed text.